Mapping Britain's Landscapes

D1646980

Rivers

Barbara Taylor

FRANKLIN WATTS

This edition published 2012 by Franklin Watts

Copyright © Franklin Watts 2012

Franklin Watts
338 Euston Road
London NW1 3BH

Franklin Watts Australia
Level 17/207 Kent Street
Sydney, NSW 2000

Series editor: Sarah Peutrill
Art director: Jonathan Hair
Design: White Design
Picture research: Diana Morris
Consultant: Steve Watts
Additional map illustrations: John Alston

A CIP catalogue record for this book is available from the British Library.

Dewey number: 526.09141
ISBN: 978 1 4451 0935 0

Printed in China

Franklin Watts is a division of Hachette Children's Books, an Hachette Livre UK company.
www.hachette.co.uk

RIVER SAFETY
Rivers can be dangerous places. Always follow the safety advice of a teacher or other adult and stay well away from fast-flowing water.

Picture credits: Altos Mapping: 9. Courtesy of the Elan Valley Visitor Centre: 25. © ESA 2003: 15. Paul Glendell/PD: 5. Jason Hawkes/Corbis: front cover, 19. John Heseltine/Corbis: 8. Richard Klune/Corbis: 20t. Mike Lane/Still Pictures: 24. Brian Moyes/PD: 22. Ordnance Survey © Crown copyright 2007: 23. Ordnance Survey © Crown copyright 2007 supplied by mapsinternational.co.uk: front cover l, 4, 11, 13, 17, 18, 21, 29. Peter Smith Photography: 16. John Sparks/Corbis: 10. Topfoto: 20b. Adam Woolfitt/Corbis: 1, 6. David Wootton/PD: 12.
Every attempt has been made to clear copyright. Should there be any inadvertent omission please apply to the publisher for rectification.

Note to parents and teachers: Every effort has been made by the Publishers to ensure that the websites in this book are suitable for children, that they are of the highest educational value, and that they contain no inappropriate or offensive material. However, because of the nature of the Internet, it is impossible to guarantee that the contents of these sites will not be altered. We strongly advise that Internet access is supervised by a responsible adult.

Contents

Mapping rivers

Rivers are channels of fresh water that flow downhill from high ground to low ground, often pouring into the sea. There are around 20,000 rivers in Britain, which flow through many types of landscape and settlement.

Maps and photographs

→ A map can tell you much more about a river than a photograph.

→ A photograph of a river is complicated and shows a lot of details, which are difficult to interpret. A map of a river is a simple picture, seen from above. It highlights important information about the river.

→ A photograph may just show you what a river looks like, while a map helps you to answer questions, such as: "How has the river changed the land?" or "How do people use the river?"

→ Photographs of rivers all have a similar style, while maps can be drawn in many ways to show different kinds of information.

MAPS AND RIVERS

Maps show us where rivers flow and how they are used. They don't show things that move around, such as boats or people, just the things that are there all the time. It's impossible to mark everything on a map, so mapmakers choose the most important features of the river. Maps use colours, lines and special shapes called symbols to mark the positions of river features. Look at the key on the side of a map to find out what the colours, lines and symbols mean.

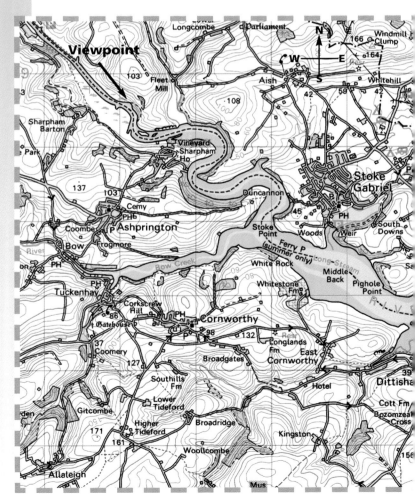

MAPS OF BRITAIN

There are many types of map, such as landscape maps, road maps, weather maps, tourist maps, world maps and maps of shopping centres. Books of maps are called atlases. You can look up places in an atlas index and find the square on the map where the place is located. (See pages 14/15 for more about finding places on maps.)

The most useful maps for finding out about Britain's river landscapes are Ordnance Survey (OS) maps, like the one opposite. This book shows you how to understand OS maps and other maps, and how they can reveal the features of rivers.

On a map, north is usually at the top, south is at the bottom, west is on the left and east is on the right. To help you remember this, make up a rhyme going clockwise around the compass, such as, "Never Enjoy Slimy Waffles".

↑ **This is the River Dart, winding its way through the countryside of South Devon, in the south west of Britain. Compare the shape of the river on the photograph with the river on the map. South is at the top of the photo but at the bottom of the map. The viewpoint is marked on the map with an arrow showing the direction.**

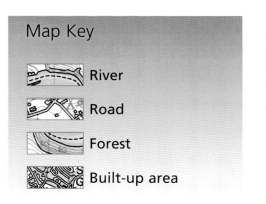

Map Key

River

Road

Forest

Built-up area

Rivers and the water cycle

The water in rivers comes from precipitation, such as rain, that falls from the sky. This makes rivers part of the water cycle, which is the movement of water from the sky to the land or sea and back to the sky again. The water cycle has no beginning and no end. It keeps recycling all the water so the amount of water on the Earth always stays the same.

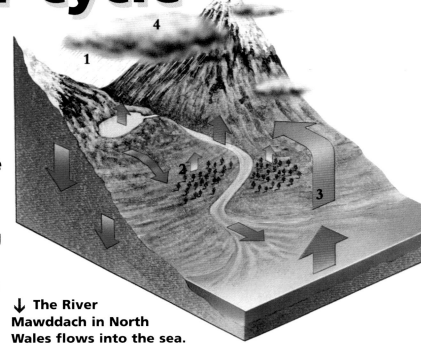

↓ The River Mawddach in North Wales flows into the sea.

LOOK AT THE DIAGRAM AND PHOTO (LEFT)

1 Precipitation falls from clouds and collects in rivers, lakes and oceans.

2 Water at the surface of rivers, lakes and oceans warms up in the Sun. Some of it turns into an invisible gas called water vapour and disappears into the air. This is called evaporation.

3 The evaporated water rises up into the air, cools down and turns back into tiny drops of liquid water. This is called condensation.

4 The condensed water drops collect together to make clouds. When the water drops become too large and heavy to hang in the sky, they fall from the clouds as precipitation. Water collects in the river, ready to begin the cycle all over again.

• Where are some of the parts of the water cycle happening in the photograph?

TAKING IT FURTHER
Look on the Internet to find out the source of five British rivers. They can be local rivers in your own area, or large rivers such as the Trent, the Severn, the Mersey, the Tweed or the Thames.

→ **On a weather map, the landscape is not so important. The main features are the symbols used to show features of the weather, such as rain, snow, clouds and sunshine. The numbers indicate the temperature in different areas.**

Where rivers start
→ **Rivers begin from rainfall. They always flow downhill from a starting point, called the source. There are four main sources of rivers:**

→ **1) A natural hollow in the land where water collects.**

→ **2) A marsh or a lake.**

→ **3) The end of a melting glacier (a river of ice).**

→ **4) Underground water that gushes out onto the surface as a spring.**

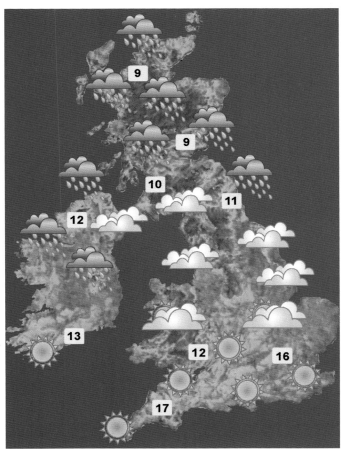

How do rivers change the land?

River water is pulled downhill by the force of gravity. As the water flows downhill, it wears away the land by loosening or breaking off pieces of rock and soil and carrying them away. This process is called erosion. The river deposits the eroded material in another place.

THE EFFECT OF RIVERS ON THE LAND

Rivers erode dips and channels in the land in some places and build up banks and new land in other places. Small streams or smaller rivers called tributaries flow into the main river channel, forming a branching pattern called a drainage pattern. The shape of this pattern depends on the rocks, soil, climate and changes people make to the course of the river.

→ **The Devil's Kitchen area of Snowdonia. The name comes from the clouds, which were said to look like cooking smoke coming out of a chimney. You can see the river water swirling around the rocks and wearing them away.**

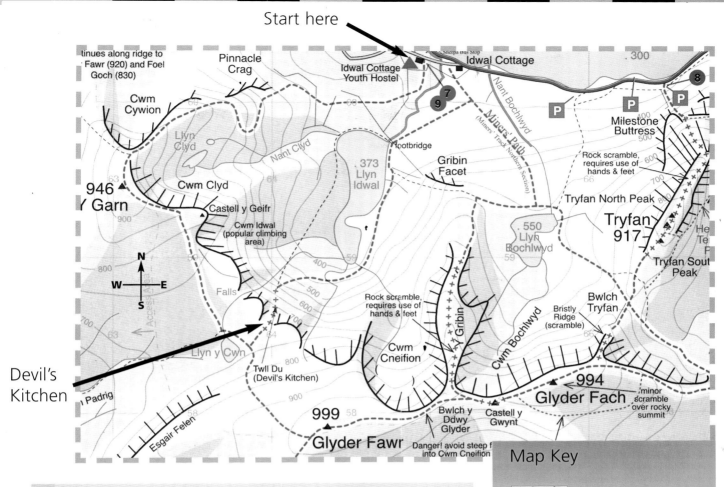

Start here

continues along ridge to
Y Fawr (920) and Foel
Goch (830)

Pinnacle
Crag

Sherpa Bus Stop

Idwal Cottage

Idwal Cottage
Youth Hostel

Cwm
Cywion

.300

8

P

P

P

Llyn
Clyd

Nant Clyd

footbridge

Milestone
Buttress

Rock scramble,
requires use of
hands & feet

Gribin
Facet

.373
Llyn
Idwal

Cwm Clyd

946
Y Garn

Tryfan North Peak

Castell y Geifr

Cwm Idwal
(popular climbing
area)

.550
Llyn
Bochlwyd

Tryfan
917

He
Te
P

Tryfan South
Peak

N
W — E
S

Falls

Rock scramble,
requires use of
hands & feet

Y Gribin

Cwm Bochlwyd

Bwlch
Tryfan

Bristly
Ridge
(scramble)

Llyn y Cwn

Cwm
Cneifion

minor
scramble
over rocky
summit

994
Glyder Fach

Twll Du
(Devil's Kitchen)

Devil's
Kitchen

Padrig

Esgair Felen

999

Glyder Fawr

Bwlch y
Ddwy
Glyder

Castell y
Gwynt

Danger! avoid steep
into Cwm Cneifion

Miner's Path

Nant Bochlwyd

(Miner's Track Northern Section)

Map Key

Footpath

Cliffs

0 km   **Scale**   1 km

0 cm   1 cm   2 cm   3 cm   4 cm

⬇ Using the map

Planning routes and looking at scale

This map of Snowdonia shows a high ridge called The Glyders, with the rivers flowing down from the ridge into a number of lakes. Plan a circular walk from the Idwal Cottage Youth Hostel, up onto the ridge through the Devil's Kitchen, along the ridge and back again.

Look at the scale on the map. This shows you how much smaller the mountains are on the map compared with their size in real life. On this map, 1 cm on the map is equal to 250 m in real life.

Maps can be drawn to different scales. Large scale maps like this one show a small area in a lot of detail. Small scale maps show a large area, with very little detail. On an electronic map, you can zoom in and out and view the map at different scales.

TAKING IT FURTHER

Find some large and small scale maps of your area. Which scale is best for the following purposes:

• investigating the rivers of Britain?
• canoeing along a river?
• planning a route by car or train?
• finding a street in a town?

Rivers in the highlands

Near the source of a river, the water flows fast down steep slopes, which are usually on higher ground or in the mountains – the highlands.

The water cuts down into the land, carving out a narrow, V-shaped channel. Other characteristic features of rivers in the highlands are waterfalls, foaming "white water" and tongues of land called spurs along the valley sides.

→ **The waterfalls of Sour Milk Gill in the Lake District flow down over a sloping cliff of hard rock. The water has worn away the softer rock below the falls so the river drops down from a great height.**

← **Three-dimensional maps show how the land goes up and down, but they can't be folded up and carried around very easily.**

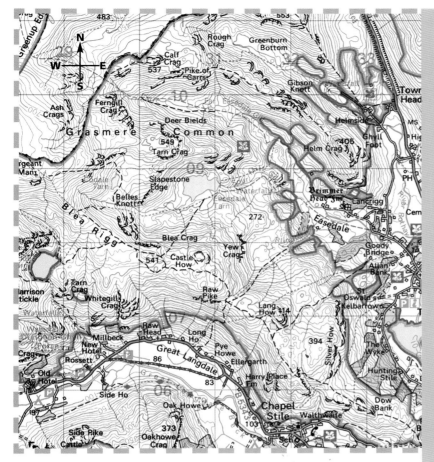

CONTOUR LINES

One of the main ways of showing the ups and downs of the land on a flat map is by using thin brown lines called contours. Contour lines join up points on the map that are the same number of metres above the sea. When contour lines are close together the slopes are very steep. In a V-shaped valley the contour lines meet at the top of the valley to make a V-shape.

TAKING IT FURTHER

Find out some other ways of showing height on a map, such as using colour shading.

Lines called hachures may also show height on a map. Find a map with hachures. Are they thicker or thinner on steeper slopes?

Look at the map

→ This map is of Grasmere Common in the Lake District.

→ Find the blue lines that show the rivers. The brown contour lines around them are close together – showing that the rivers are in steeply sloping valleys.

→ The thick, jagged black lines in some areas mark the edges of rocky cliffs, called crags. Can you find Blea Crag and Yew Crag?

→ The waterfalls in the photograph are in Sour Milk Gill, a valley leading down from Easedale Tarn. Find the waterfalls on the map.

→ Can you imagine what the landscape would look like if you walked up Far Easedale Gill?

→ The height at a particular point on a map is sometimes marked by a spot height. There is one of these spot heights just below Sour Milk Gill. How many metres high is the land at this point?

Rivers in the lowlands

As a river flows from the highlands onto lower ground, it starts to twist and turn, forming loops called meanders. The river cuts sideways into the land, rather than downwards as it did in the highlands. Lots of small streams have now joined the river so the river is wider and flows through a deep channel.

THE RIVER DEE

The best way to see a river's meanders is in an aerial photograph like this. The map opposite shows the same river, but there is more of the river shown on the map. The small box on the map shows the area you can see on the photograph.

MEANDERS

When the curve of a river changes direction, it is the start of a new meander. On the outside bend of a meander, the river flows quickly. It eats into the riverbank, carrying material away and forming small cliffs. On the inside bend, the river water flows more slowly. It drops, or deposits, some of the material it is carrying to make ridges of sand and gravel, called bars. Since one riverbank is cut away at the same time as the other bank is filled in, the width of the river stays roughly the same.

Map Key

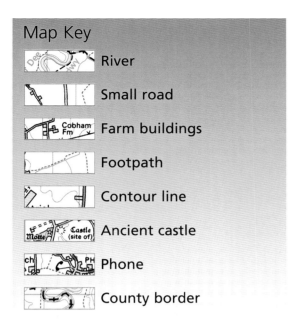

River	
Small road	
Farm buildings	
Footpath	
Contour line	
Ancient castle	
Phone	
County border	

← **The meanders of the River Dee, near Wrexham in Wales.**

⬇ Using the map

Symbols

A map uses simple symbols to pick out the main features of an area such as rivers or lakes, as well as features people have built, such as farms and towns. Symbols are simple signs, lines, letters or coloured areas that stand for the real things.

The key (left) shows some of the symbols used on this map of the River Dee. Find each one on the map.

Can you match the River Dee's meanders in the photograph with the meanders on the map?

The border between Wales and England mainly follows the course of the river. Why do you think this is? Why does it sometimes follow a slightly different route?

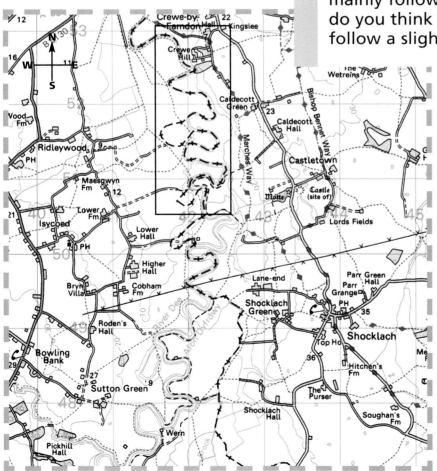

TAKING IT FURTHER

Find the River Dee in an atlas. Can you name the mountains where it starts and the sea that it flows into?

Follow the River Dee from Farndon (off the top of this map) down to Bangor on Dee (off the bottom of this map). How many meanders can you count on this stretch of the river?

13

Where rivers meet the sea

Most rivers end by flowing into the sea. This wide opening is called the river's mouth. If the mouth is very wide, it is also called an estuary. Here, the salty seawater pushes its way up the river with the tide.

DROPPING MATERIAL

At the mouth the river slows down and drops the particles of sand, gravel and mud that it is carrying. This mud builds up to make mud flats beside the river.

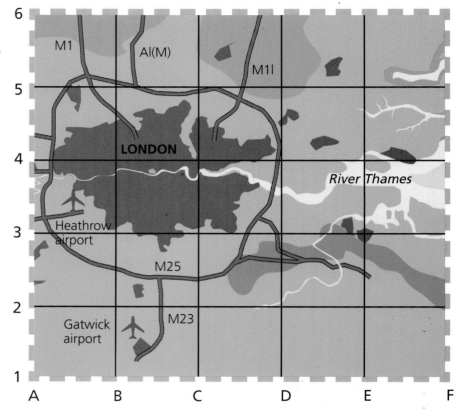

↑ This sketch map is based on the photograph of the River Thames, opposite. It is a simplified version of the photograph, which makes it much easier to see where things are.

↓ Using the map

Grid references

The map is divided into squares by lines called grid lines. At the end of each grid line is a number or a letter. Grid references help to pinpoint a particular square on the map. They always have the number or letter of the line at the top or bottom of the map first, then the number or letter of the line up the sides of the map. You can remember this by thinking of the phrase: "along the corridor and up the stairs". For example Heathrow Airport is in square A3.

Give the grid reference for the square where the estuary of the River Thames meets the M25.

TAKING IT FURTHER

Find the River Thames in an atlas and trace its journey from its source in the Cotswolds of Gloucestershire to the North Sea. The Thames is the longest river in England and millions of people depend on its waters. Find out the total length of the River Thames. Which six counties does the river flow through?

Why do you think the City of London grew up beside the River Thames?

Look at the photograph

→ This photograph was made from three photographs that show the River Thames flowing through London and into the North Sea. Each photograph has been given a different colour. The photographs were taken from high above the ground looking straight down.

→ Find the big meanders along the river. Where does the river flow into the sea?

→ Can you find two other rivers that flow into the North Sea near the estuary of the River Thames? Look in an atlas to find out their names.

When rivers flood

Sometimes a river gets too full so some of the water spills over the riverbanks and floods the land nearby. This usually happens in the lowlands, where rivers flow across flatter land, called the river's floodplain. Floods damage crops, buildings and bridges and put the lives of people and animals at risk.

WHY DO FLOODS HAPPEN?

- Very heavy rainfall or a lot of snow melting suddenly in spring.
- High tides on the coast causing flooding at the mouth of a river.
- People making changes to the natural course of a river, such as cutting down lots of trees, or draining marshes which soak up water.
- Water draining quickly from concrete surfaces in towns and cities and filling up rivers too fast.

↑ **A flooded section of the River Ouse in York in 2000. The floods were caused by extreme weather.**

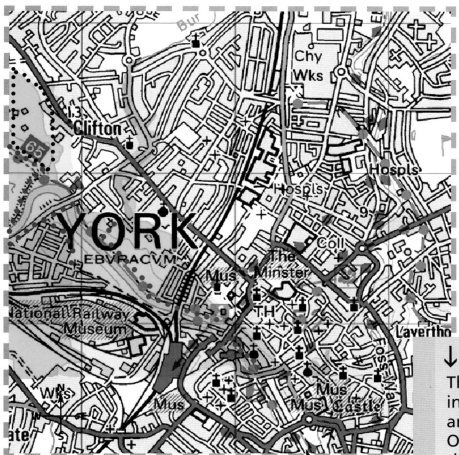

Visit the Environment Agency website and investigate flood risk maps for your area. Go to: www.environment-agency.gov.uk/homeandleisure/floods/31650.aspx and type in your postcode. You could also create a project folder on severe floods in recent years.

↑ **Maps, like this one of York, predict the risk of flooding. They help people to plan for future floods and decide where to build houses or factories and farm the land safely.**

River Ouse

THE RIVER OUSE

Most of Britain was affected by severe floods in the autumn of 2000, especially in city centres where bridges cross rivers. In York, the floods were the highest for over 350 years. The River Ouse burst its banks after heavy rain and the floodwater caused major damage to hundreds of buildings. Special flood defence walls and thousands of sandbags held back the water, but many people had to be rescued from their homes by boat. The railway line between York and Darlington had to be closed when floods from the River Ouse and the River Derwent covered the railway tracks.

↓ Look at the map

This map provides information about flood risks and flood defences. The River Ouse is just north and east of the Railway Museum.

Dark blue shows the natural floodplain area that could be flooded if there were no flood defences.

Green shows the extent of a future extreme flood.

The red line shows flood defences, such as walls, embankments and areas to store floodwater.

The black-dotted area near Clifton has flood defences in place. Without the defences, this area would be flooded.

River settlements

In the past people often settled near rivers because they can be used in so many different ways. Small settlements often grew up at places where rivers were easy to cross or where a river bend surrounded a village, making it easy to defend. Many of these small settlements have grown into Britain's towns and cities.

Look at the photo and map

→ This map of Marlow has been turned so that it faces the same way as the photo. North on the map is now down the left hand side. Which way is the river flowing?

→ Find Marlow's famous suspension bridge in the photo and on the map.

→ Turn the book to look closely at the map symbols. Where is the weir on the river? And the same on the photo?

→ Can you find a school, a church and a railway station on the map?

→ What leisure interests could you follow in Marlow?

WHY LIVE NEAR RIVERS?
- People can use the water for drinking and washing.
- Farmers can water their crops or provide water for their farm animals to drink. Crops grow well on the rich soils of river floodplains. These soils are built up from layers of river mud, which the river deposits along its banks in times of flood.
- Fast-flowing rivers can be used to drive machinery or generate electricity (see pages 24–25).

- Rivers are water highways, useful for transporting goods and people.
- People use rivers in their leisure time for activities such as canoeing and fishing.
- At the mouth of some rivers, sheltered, deep-water sites make ideal ports or harbours for fishing, trade or industry.

↑ **This is the town of Marlow, on the River Thames in Buckinghamshire, southern England. Marlow grew up around a bridge over the river and was on a major trade route from London, with barges carrying goods such as corn, oil, paper and wood along the river.**

FLOOD RISKS

The first settlements were usually built away from marshy areas or places that might flood. Today, there are so many people living in Britain that more and more homes have to be built in areas at risk from river flooding. People also like to build their homes on the flat land near rivers, with a pleasant view.

Transport and crossing places

Rivers and canals have been used for transporting people and goods for centuries. However, rivers are also barriers to journeys. Small rivers can be crossed at shallow places called fords. Deeper and wider rivers have to be crossed using ferries, bridges or tunnels.

SatNav

Satellite navigation systems are a special kind of map. In cars they pinpoint exactly where you are by picking up radio signals sent out by a network of satellites out in space. They can be used instead of road maps like the one opposite.

↑ The Mersey ferries transport over half a million passengers every year and are a popular tourist attraction.

THE RIVER MERSEY

Liverpool grew up at the mouth of the River Mersey, where it flows into the Irish Sea. People have been crossing the River Mersey from Liverpool to Birkenhead by ferry for over 800 years. Nowadays, as well as the ferries there are also three tunnels underneath the river, which provide an alternative means of crossing.

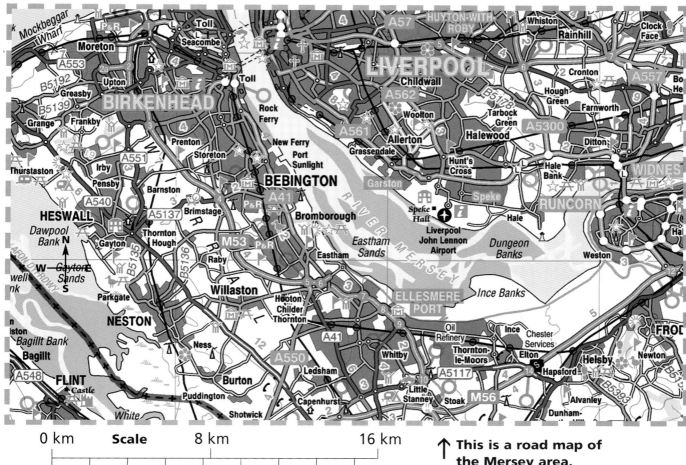

Scale

0 km   8 km   16 km

0 cm   1 cm   2 cm   3 cm   4 cm   5 cm   6 cm   7 cm   8 cm

↑ **This is a road map of the Mersey area.**

↓ Using the map

Maps help you find your way to places. If you are going on a journey, it's a good idea to plan your route on a map.

Find the narrow crossing place where the ferries and tunnels cross the Mersey. Imagine all these crossings are not in use. How long would it take you to go all the way round by road, crossing the river at the Runcorn-Widnes bridge? Some of the roads will be A roads and some will be motorways. Measure the total distance using a piece of wool or thin string and a ruler. Then use the map scale to convert this figure into the distance in the real place.

Think about the average speed of a car on these roads and calculate the time the journey takes.

TAKING IT FURTHER

The River Mersey starts near Stockport and flows westwards for about 112 km until it reaches Liverpool. Trace the course of the River Mersey on an atlas. Look at the map symbols to find out more about the features along the riverbanks. How many settlements are built near the river? Where are the main bridges?

Water and work

Many of the jobs people do are closely linked to rivers, from farming, forestry and conservation to shipbuilding, power generation and the housing industry. Many heavy industries that used to be located next to urban riversides, such as shipbuilding, have declined and these parts of Britain's rivers are now mainly used for the leisure and tourist industry.

↓ The *Cardigan Bay* warship being built for the British Royal Navy at the BAE Systems shipyard on the River Clyde.

THE RIVER CLYDE, GLASGOW

The River Clyde is the third longest river in Scotland. It was very important during the Industrial Revolution for trade with the Americas. The river channel was dredged to make it deeper and wider so large ships could navigate all the way into Glasgow. Shipbuilding became the most important industry on the river, with warships and ocean liners being built there.

After the Second World War (1939–45), fewer warships were needed and other shipbuilding countries took work away from the Clyde shipbuilders. Many shipyards closed but today there are still two major shipyards on the Clyde, which make warships such as the one in the photograph.

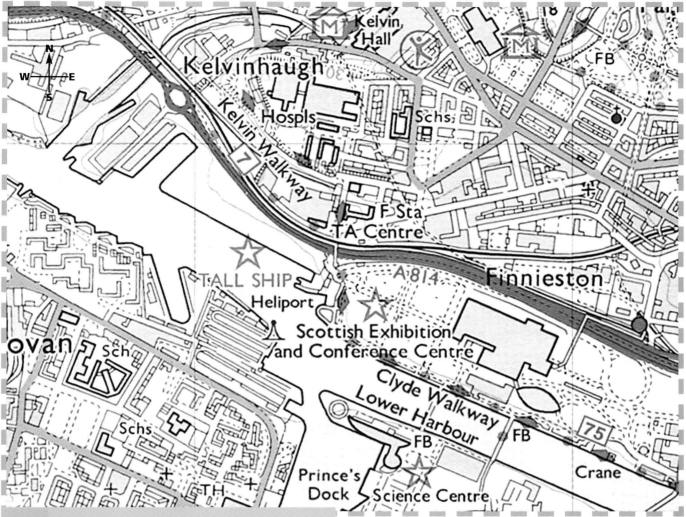

Look at the map

→ **This map shows part of the River Clyde flowing through the docklands of Glasgow.**

→ **Find the following visitor attractions on the map:**
  - **Scottish Exhibition and Conference Centre**
  - **Tall Ship**
  - **Crane**
  - **Museum**

→ **What other future uses for the old docklands can you think of?**

CLYDE REDEVELOPMENT

Other dockland areas where ships once unloaded their cargoes are now being used for office blocks, housing, shopping and tourist attractions. The river has also been cleaned up over the last 20 years to make it suitable for leisure use.

TAKE IT FURTHER

Find out where the River Clyde begins and ends. Find out about the Glasgow Harbour development using the Internet.

Dams and reservoirs

Dams are very strong, thick walls built across river valleys to control the flow of water. The large lakes that form behind the dams are called reservoirs and they are marked as patches of blue on maps, just like natural lakes. The water stored in the reservoir can be released when it is needed.

↓ The Claerwen Dam in Wales took six years to build and was finished in 1952. It is 56 m high and 355 m long. The reservoir behind the dam holds 483,000 megalitres of water. When the reservoir is full, water overflows down the face of the dam, making a striking waterfall.

BRITISH DAMS

There are about 2,500 large dams in Britain. They are used to control flooding, generate electricity (hydro-power) and provide a regular water supply for houses, farms, industry and leisure activities on rivers.

THE ELAN VALLEY DAMS

The four massive dams on the Elan and Claerwen Rivers in Mid Wales were built at the beginning of the 20th century to provide water for the city of Birmingham. At the end of the 20th century, five new hydro-power turbines were hidden underground at the bottom of the original dams to generate electricity. The area is famous for its scenery and wildlife, such as red kites (birds).

USE AN ATLAS

In an atlas, find the Elan Valley reservoirs in the Cambrian Mountains of Mid Wales. The reservoirs are south east of Aberystwyth, which is in the middle of Cardigan Bay. Look for Llyn (Lake) Brianne, which is south of the Claerwen Reservoir. Which river flows into Llyn Brianne from the north?

Map legend:
- Woodland
- Reservoirs
- Estate Boundary and Watershed
- Roads

Map labels: River Elan, Abergwngu, River Gwngu, River Elan, Pont ar Elan, Nant Hirin, Craig Goch Reservoir, A 470 To Llangurig, To Worcester A44, River Claerwen, Pen-y-Garreg Reservoir, B4518, Rhayader, Filter beds, Claerwen Reservoir, Garreg-Ddu Viaduct, Elan Village, River Wye, A470 To Builth Wells, Elan Valley Visitor Centre, River Claerwen, Nant-y-Carw, Caban Coch Reservoir, Rhiwnant, Dol y Mynach Dam

Look at the map

→ **Is the Claerwen Reservoir east or west of the Caban Coch Reservoir?**

→ **Is the visitor centre north or south of the Craig Coch Reservoir? Which is the most southerly reservoir?**

TAKING IT FURTHER

Hydro-power provides at least 10% of Scotland's energy. Find out about big hydro-power schemes in Scotland such as the Glendoe hydro-power scheme.

Building a dam across a river changes the natural flow of water. What sort of problems do you think this might cause? Think about the effects on wildlife and farming. When the river flows into the reservoir behind the dam, what happens to all the mud and stones it is carrying?

Rivers and recreation

From canoeing, rowing and fishing to cycling, painting and photography, many people in Britain choose to spend their leisure time on or near rivers. People enjoy seeing river features, such as waterfalls or the wildlife that depends on rivers.

PICTORIAL MAPS

Many tourist maps of rivers are drawn in a pictorial style. This means that little pictures are used to stand for the different leisure features, such as sailing, picnic sites, nature reserves or places to hire boats or bicycles.

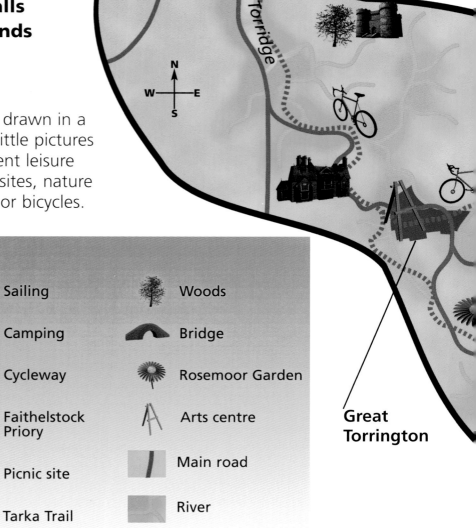

Instow

Northam

Bideford

River Torridge

Great Torrington

Map Key

Country estate	Sailing	Woods	
Lifeguard	Camping	Bridge	
Castle	Cycleway	Rosemoor Garden	
Country estate	Faithelstock Priory	Arts centre	
Ferry (Summer only)	Picnic site	Main road	
	Tarka Trail	River	

TIPS ON DRAWING PICTORIAL MAPS:

- This sort of map can be creative, decorative and fun. It doesn't have to be too accurate, just give a general idea of things to do along the river.
- The edge of the map can even be an unusual shape, such as the outline of an otter shown on these two pages.
- Don't worry about scale. The features can be much bigger than they would be on a landscape map.
- Make the picture symbols three dimensional, as if you were looking at them from the ground, not from above.
- Draw simple pictures of things with bold lines, not just outline shapes. The symbols can even be in a cartoon style.
  - Don't include too much detail in the background. Make the pictorial symbols stand out and become the main focus of the map.
    - You could include boxes around the edge of the map with photographs or drawings of each site and more details, such as telephone numbers and opening times.
    - Include a key so people using the map can understand your symbols.

↓ Using the map

The map shows the River Torrington in north-west Devon. Beside the river is the Tarka Trail – a walking and cycling trail beside parts of the river featured in Henry Williamson's book, *Tarka the Otter*.

Which town is near the historical bridge across the river? Where is Rosemoor Garden? Where can you catch a ferry across the river? Where can you camp? Which is the best spot to see the biggest river meanders?

TAKING IT FURTHER

Using an atlas, choose a river in Britain, such as the Thames through London or the Tyne in Newcastle, where there are lots of tourist attractions. Draw a pictorial map of a stretch of the river.

Check your map skills

Use these two pages to check that you understand the mapping skills introduced in this book. Once you can read a map, you will be able to discover all sorts of information about rivers and how they change the landscape.

SCALE

Everything on a map is usually reduced down by the same amount to fit onto the map. This is called drawing to scale. The scale of a map tells you how the size of the map compares to the size of the real landscape. You can use the scale to work out the distances between two or more points on the map.

GRIDS

A map grid is a network of equal squares drawn on top of the map. At the edge of a map, each line has a number or a letter at the end. To give a grid reference, find the numbers or letters at the ends of the two lines that meet in the bottom left-hand corner of a grid square. Refer to the line that goes up and down the map first (the numbers or letters along the bottom), then the line that goes from side to side (the numbers along the side). So Dimple is in square 2960.

Look at the map

→ Look carefully at the map of Matlock, which is on the River Derwent, in Derbyshire. The River Derwent is the longest river in the Peak District. Answer these questions about the map.

→ What is the name of the station nearest to the river?

→ What runs alongside most of the river?

→ Where is the best place to drive across the river?

→ Where would a tourist be able to find information about the area?

→ Where is the biggest river meander? Give a grid reference to this square on the map.

→ Why do you think most of the settlement is on the north side of the river?

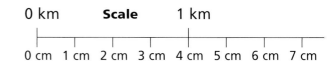

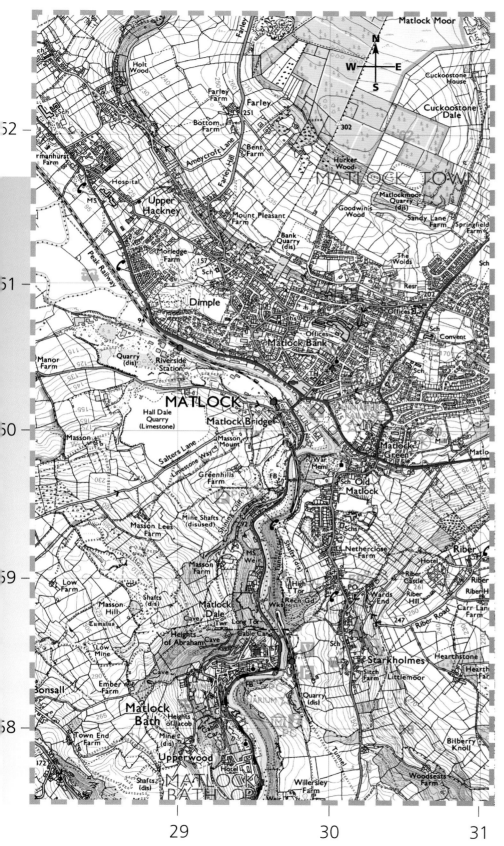

Map Key

Tourist information

Main road

Train station

Contour line

SYMBOLS

Map symbols bring a map to life. They are simple signs that show where things are on a map. A list called a key or a legend on the edge of the map explains what the symbols stand for.

HEIGHT

The ups and downs of the land can be shown on a flat map by pictures of hills, shading, coloured areas or lines called hachures. The main way of showing height on a map is usually by contour lines. These are brown lines that join up places that are the same height above sea level. When the contours are close together, the land is steep. When the contours are far apart, the land is flatter. Rings of contours, one inside the other, show hills or mountains.

Britain's rivers

This map shows some of the major rivers of Britain. It also shows all the rivers mentioned in this book.

N
W E
S

Thurso

Spey

Dee

SCOTLAND Tay

Forth

NORTH SEA

Tweed

Clyde

Tyne

Eden

Ribble

Derwent

IRISH SEA

Ouse

Mersey Derwent

Trent

Dee

ENGLAND

Rheidol

Great Ouse

Severn

Little Ouse

Mawddach

Avon

Elan

Claerwen Wye

Thames

WALES

Severn

Torrington

Stour

Test

Medway

Exe

Tamar

Dart

ENGLISH CHANNEL

Glossary

Atlas A book of maps.

Aerial photograph A photograph taken from the sky looking down on the land.

Canal A man-made waterway (often fairly straight) used for transport or watering crops.

Condensation The process by which a gas (such as water vapour) changes into a liquid (such as liquid water) when it cools down.

Contour A line on a map which joins places that are the same height above sea level.

Dam A large wall or bank built across a river to hold back the water.

Drainage pattern The arrangement of a river and its tributaries across the land, seen from above.

Erosion The loosening of rocks and soil and the carrying away of this material by the wind, water or ice.

Estuary The wide mouth of a river where freshwater in the river mixes with the salty water of the sea.

Evaporation The process by which a liquid changes into a gas (such as water vapour) when it is heated.

Ferry A place where people or goods are carried across water, such as a river, in a boat.

Floodplain The wide, flat valley floor of a lowland river, which is often flooded by the river water.

Ford A shallow area of water that may be crossed by wading, riding or driving through the water.

Gill A narrow mountain stream or a deep valley.

Glacier A large mass of ice on high ground, which flows slowly downhill.

Great Britain A country that includes England, Wales and Scotland.

Grid lines Lines forming a network of squares on a map, which help to locate points on the map easily and accurately.

Hachure A short, thick line used on maps to show the steepness and direction of slopes.

Hydro-power Electrical power generated by water making turbine wheels move. ("Hydro" means water.)

Key A list that explains what the symbols on a map stand for. A key is sometimes called a legend because it tells the story of the map.

Lock A narrow section of a river with gates at either end. Inside the lock, boats can be raised or lowered by changing the water level.

Meander A large bend or loop in the course of a river, named after the River Meander in Turkey.

Megalitre One million litres.

Mouth The end of a river, where it flows into the sea or a lake.

Ordnance Survey An organisation that makes accurate and detailed maps of the UK.

Precipitation All forms of water falling out of clouds to the Earth including rain, snow, hail and sleet.

Reservoir A lake made when people dam a river. A reservoir stores water for drinking, watering crops or making electricity.

Scale The number of units of measurement on the ground represented by a certain number of units on a map.

Sediment Small particles of rocks, soil or living things that are carried along and deposited (dropped) by the river.

Settlement A place where people build their homes and settle down to live their lives.

Spot height A point on a map where the exact height of the land is marked.

Spring A place where water comes up to the surface and pours out to form a stream.

Tarn A small lake.

Tributary A small stream or river that flows into a bigger stream or river.

Waterfall A point where a river suddenly drops over a "step" of rock and forms a curtain of falling water.

Weir A dam across a river to regulate the flow of water.

Index

FURTHER INFORMATION WEBSITES:

Websites on maps
Ordnance Survey:
http://mapzone.ordnancesurvey.co.uk/mapzone/
http://maps.google.co.uk/
Type in place names or postcodes to see aerial views and maps of places in Britain.

Websites about the environment:
Environment Agency: http://www.environment-agency.gov.uk/homeandleisure/floods/
The National Trust: www.nationaltrust.org.uk

Websites about rivers:
http://woodlands-junior.kent.sch.uk/riverthames/facts.htm
www.timbosliverpool.co.uk/mersey/index.htm
www.vagavalley.co.uk/elanvalley.htm
www.bbc.co.uk/devon/discovering/rivers/torridge/shtml
www.derbyshireuk.net/river derwent.html
www.sln.org.uk/trentweb/default.htm

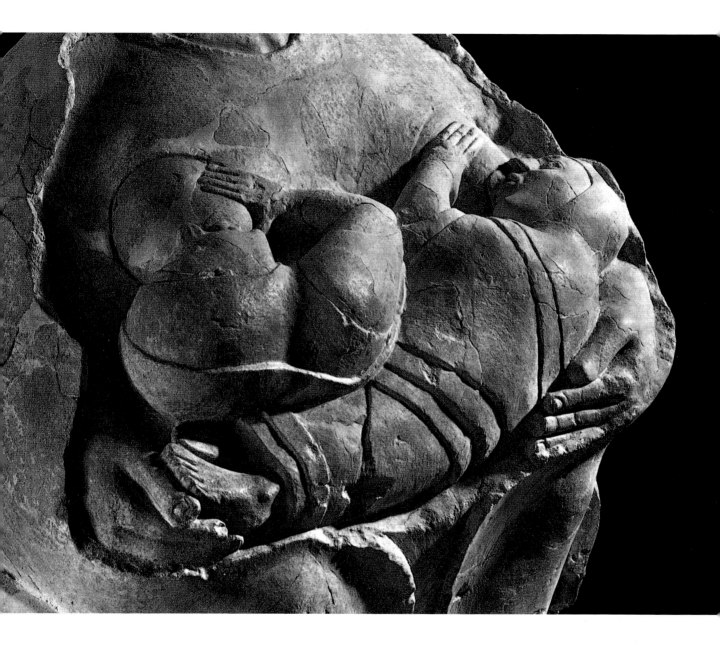

While the image of Madonna and Child has become universal through Christian iconography, representations of a virgin mother suckling twins are far less familiar. (Mother Goddess with twins, terracotta figure, Roman, c. 300 AD).

It is well-known, however, that the image of Isis suckling Horus in Egyptian art demonstrates the Madonna motif centuries before the Christian era; and Horus is clearly a twin deity, as his rivalry with Set confirms.

As the image of living nature that gives birth to all creatures, the virgin mother-goddess is often idealized into an all-embracing, all-nurturing power. Nature does not nurture her offspring impartially, however. She takes sides and favours the stronger; yet in a rare instance when the weaker manages to triumph, the credit still goes to nature herself. The 'odds of survival' are extremely ambiguous, and twins, ultimately unequal in their will to survive, will at first be quite indistinguishable, both writhing and plucking with equal hunger at their mother's breasts. (Kourotrophos, Goddess Suckling Twins)

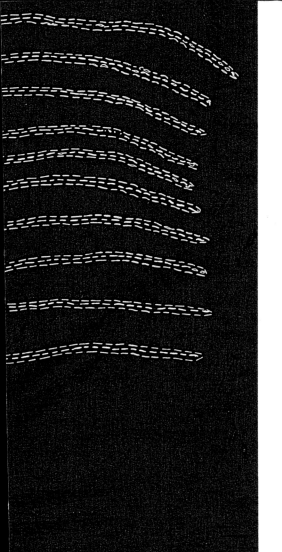

Through the ages, the tabu on twins in aboriginal cultures in Africa and North and South America, has been preserved as one of the strongest of all. (Twins suckling mother figure, Asafo flag, Ghana)

It is the way of the Sacred to conceal itself (except in rare cases) from direct revelation, to disclose its forces through signs and events which may then be reproduced, mimetically, in song, ritual, cultic practices and observances. But when twins appear, the Sacred is revealed directly: we are blinded by our inability to distinguish One from Other and therefore open to penetration by occult forces such as those that unfold in biological twinning and genetic replication. Sedna, the Eskimo Ocean Goddess, is a veritable glyph of biological generation: half sperm, half ovum, filled with zygotic eggs, she nurses her two-headed progeny, a primitive effigy of Siamese twins. (Stone-cut print, 1961)

The earliest clear-cut representations of human soul resurrection appear in Egyptian tomb paintings, showing the *ba* as a winged phoenix hovering over the mummified corpse. (Papyrus of Ani, 19th Dynasty scroll)

But resurrection is only one half of the twin function of the soul-double, which can also appear as a mesmerizing harpy or vampire. Merging with the double results in total devitalization and death, but untimely separation from it can also be fatal. It must remain vitally linked with the body. Here primitive psychology may exhibit a deeper grasp of 'good and evil' than its modern counterpart. We are reminded that the immortal part of the soul is not all good simply for being immortal. In fact, that in us which can outlive us can also drain the very life from us while we are still alive. What is sacred also assumes the ways of violence. It is no slight thing, indeed, that 'evil' is 'live' spelled backwards. (Edvard Munch, *Harpy*, lithograph, 1900)

If dyadic perception is truly primary to the primitive (i.e., original, pre-logical) perception of the world, nowhere is the evidence more clear than in the mythology of First Parents represented as Twins. In countless symbolic and figurative expressions, primitive intuition discloses what we now designate scientifically as the structure of DNA, the parenting substance of all organic life. The ancestor couple from Maketu in the Bay of Plenty, New Zealand, are limbically entwined like the coils of DNA: as if genes had faces and bodies, so that they might reveal themselves as supernatural entities, which indeed they must have done in the numinous moment of atavistic vision. Likewise, the Chinese Adam and Eve, Fu Hsi and Nu Kua, exhibit long entwining tails, perfect image of the double helix as a kind of dyadic *kundalini*. While we can only imagine the immense replicating potency of the DNA–RNA complex as it writhes and dances in our very skins, the primitive seer or the ancient shaman were able to participate directly in the somatic realm *and* bring it through into conscious perception. The identity of the First Parents had to be known and remembered, for every tribe and clan, every lineage be it sacred or profane, was known to emerge from Them, the numinous life-ground. As the Na Khi, a Tibetan people of southeastern China, have put it: 'We must remember the origin of the medicine, or else it cannot work its magic.' Here is the true significance of the custom of revering the ancestors.

With their uncanny sense for the transposition of twinning powers, the Aztecs place the image of their Flayed God, Xipe Totec, on the *inner face* of a ceremonial mask: so that the priest who wears the mask must literally face the sacrificial double as he dances, blind, in the

flayed skin of the sacrificed victim. While the mask-mouth screams in silent agony, Xipe Totec blows the sacred current of somatic force (*mana, ecehatl*) directly into the 'third eye' of the celebrant.

Ancestors carry the sacred current of human identity through time. In ceremonial and funerary art they are represented as living in our very bones, for the skeleton (*left*) is not so much an image of life dead-and-gone, as of life gone before supporting life that comes after. (Malu-board from Eastern Iatmul, probably 19th century)

In the mirror of consciousness we see ourselves, but do we like what we see? In *Being and Nothingness*, Sartre called our typical self-mirroring 'a reflective scissiparity': the mirror interface of cross-sectioned equals. While such reflection is certainly the prerequisite of self-awareness, it is often a poor basis for self-love. Primitive psychology dramatically acknowledges this dilemma in the figure and fate of Narcissus who became enamoured of his own image and finally wasted away. (Caravaggio, *Narcissus*)

There is some unstated principle, it seems, controlling the interplay of self-love and self-hatred in us. In one respect, self-love is healthy and vitalizing. The primary narcissism of the infant foregrounds all later moments of self-worth, and when this narcissism is not fostered the result is a set of pathological disturbances. On the other hand, when the necessary dynamic of narcissism becomes too strong it can twist the entire psyche into an agon of homo-erotic obsession and tortuous self-loathing. (Francis Bacon, *Portrait of George Dyer in a Mirror*, 1967–8)

As self-reflective beings, we are all twins caught in a love/hate relationship with ourselves. There is no way out but there is a perennial temptation to go 'through the looking-glass' and merge with the Other as reflected self. The greater challenge, perhaps, is simply to face ourselves in full acceptance of both our lovable and detestable traits, our beauty and our flaws.

Robert Louis Stevenson, well-known for his adventure tales for children, may have been inspired to write *The Strange Case of Dr Jekyll and Mr Hyde* (1886) by encountering his own double in a dream. Perennially fascinated by the battle between good and evil in the human soul, generations of audiences have been spellbound by film versions of the harrowing tale. In one version of 1932, the benevolent Dr Jekyll confronts the apparition of his Double in the fireplace, mocking and defying him. An equally tormented relationship exists between Dorian Gray and his Double, described in Oscar Wilde's famous novella of 1891 (seen here in a later film). Significantly, Dorian Gray does not paint his own portrait: perhaps this is Wilde's ultimate comment on what must happen to anyone who does not assume full responsibility for creating his own personality. Wilde elevated narcissistic self-love to an aesthetic principle and used the example of Dorian Gray to show what can happen when self-love goes wrong, blinding us utterly to morality and compassion.

In the physical appearance of identical twins, we are forcibly struck by the riddle of Alterity, or Otherness: we see two distinct beings, with no way to tell which is the 'one' and which is the 'other'.

This impression is startling to a profound degree, because it both contradicts and confirms our innate sense of being the 'one' as opposed to the 'other', (i.e., everything and everyone in the world *except* us).

The twin is a shadow figure or, one might say, the embodiment of whatever we tend to deny or repress. Where either half of the asymmetry dominates, the other half becomes suppressed. But the

disparity between twins – one stronger, one weaker, one favoured, one disfavoured, etc. – may or may not be evident in the actual appearance of the pair. This very ambiguity once again illustrates the baffling and elusive character of twinhood. The mother on the right of the portrait may be more stern, perhaps less happy, than the one on the left. As we struggle to make the distinction, the mind locks into a kind of sorting mode, the same function it typically uses to confirm our sense of being 'this' rather than 'that'. (Portrait of the Cholmondeley sisters, c. 1600)

Aristophanes proposed that human lovers are twin halves of a split whole seeking to re-unite into one entity. Visual versions of the theme, such as Munch's woodcut, *The Kiss* (1897–1902), often preserve the radical ambiguity of twinning between lovers: it is impossible to tell if the two figures joined in the embrace are merged into one, giving up all separate boundaries, or just holding back from full and final interfusion. Brancusi's version of the kiss in stone (1908) shows the twinned soul-lovers melded into a monolithic unit, yet retaining a single bounding (sex, identity, Self/Other).

Encountering the double is a terrifying experience. Dante Gabriel Rossetti captures the terror vividly in his small watercolour of two lovers who meet their doubles in the flesh. (*How They Met Themselves*, 1864)

Supernatural apparitions were a popular subject in the Romantic and Gothic literature of his time.

It is one thing to encounter the double from without, another to acknowledge its present from within. In Klimt's *Pallas Athene* (1898) the gold breastplate of the goddess bears an image of the Medusa, before whose gaze we are frozen as we would be before the apparition of the double. The glaring gorgon represents the chthonic powers of nature within. For Klimt, Athene embodies the dual and ambivalent nature of art as a source of lofty vision or an agent of degeneration, exactly parallel to the role of the double in archaic psychology.

The human face is a twin twice over. It has a right and a left side which, photographed frontally, cut down the middle and pasted together, will yield two distinct faces, each one slightly different from our face as nature has composed it. In addition, there are frontal and profile views, depicted simultaneously in Picasso's portrait of Dora Maar, 1937. It also has a set of profiles, near-identical twins to each other. In Angus McBean's self-portrait, the artist makes the eye seen in three-quarter profile, on the right, match the eye seen frontally on the left, exactly duplicating Picasso. With profile-eye and frontal eye aligned, the artist, looking out from the photograph, both sees and does not see us at the same time.

The possibilities here are endless, for the elusive mutability of the human face consists in its perpetual attempt to catch a glimpse of itself. Nature has so designed it, however, that the twin who sees through the eyes remains forever distinct from the twin displayed in the face. As lookers who cannot know how we look except by reflection from the Other, we are all condemned to be twins.

In mythological terms, what characterizes the modern world is the dominance of 'person' as a fixed and exclusive entity. Largely owing to the bias of Christian theology, we have come to revere the person as singular and unique, the 'one' who possesses or embodies an immortal soul not present in any 'other'. Indeed, we are fanatically attached to this precious conception of ourselves.

But among the ancient Egyptians, as well as the Eskimos of Vancouver Island today, 'person' is not an exclusionary entity but a metamorphic power capable of self-extension, replication and bilocation. As such, its character is dyadic: two things in one. The person of the Egyptian pharaoh, for instance, is a replication of the totemic deity he represents and after which he is named: Amon I, II, III, and so on. The roman numeral attached to the deific title indicates the epochal continuity in which the incarnating god replicates itself over and over again in the person of successive human counterparts. By contrast to our stifling, one-dimensional concept of the person, this view is truly awe-engendering. Here the totemic image of the Ram-god, Amon, looms over the figure of the pharaoh.

In addition to the hierarchical form of the God-image, the totemic double can also frequently appear as the *nahual* or animal familiar of the shaman or witch. In the same way that the pharaoh 'impersonates' the deity, the shaman can assume the form of his double, can in fact impersonate a raven, salmon or bear. The shaman thus assumes the special faculties and 'animal powers' inherent to his totemic counterpart. (Totemic eagle, Kwakiutl)

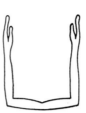

The wooden statue of King Hor Awibre from Dahshur, c. 1760 BC, is typical of Egyptian funerary art. Here the divine ancestor is represented, not so much as a human form, rather as the form of the everlasting double, the *ka*. Crowning his head, a wooden replica of the glyph for the *ka* embraces heaven in a gesture of awestruck submission. The hands convey with uncanny force the hieratic attitude of the King, transpersonal agent of the sacred in human guise.

In contrast to this sublime embodiment there is the more common modern condition of spiritual sequestration. Why is it that confined to a cell or caught in a moment of solitary agony, we look into our hands for support? In Herbert Bayer's photocollage, *Lonely Metropolitan* (1932), the hands look back from eyes planted like stigmata in the palms. Here we sense the grief rather than the exaltation of embodiment, the pain of our exile in the flesh. The Nubian king strides forward with the poise and confidence of someone who knows his counterpart exists and sustains him.

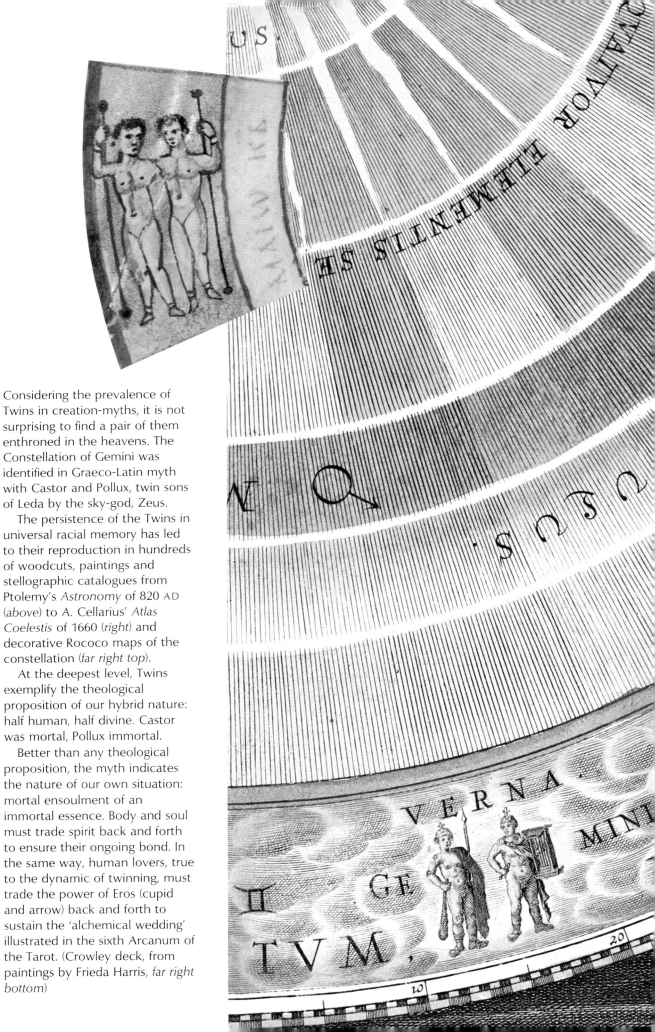

Considering the prevalence of Twins in creation-myths, it is not surprising to find a pair of them enthroned in the heavens. The Constellation of Gemini was identified in Graeco-Latin myth with Castor and Pollux, twin sons of Leda by the sky-god, Zeus.

The persistence of the Twins in universal racial memory has led to their reproduction in hundreds of woodcuts, paintings and stellographic catalogues from Ptolemy's *Astronomy* of 820 AD (*above*) to A. Cellarius' *Atlas Coelestis* of 1660 (*right*) and decorative Rococo maps of the constellation (*far right top*).

At the deepest level, Twins exemplify the theological proposition of our hybrid nature: half human, half divine. Castor was mortal, Pollux immortal.

Better than any theological proposition, the myth indicates the nature of our own situation: mortal ensoulment of an immortal essence. Body and soul must trade spirit back and forth to ensure their ongoing bond. In the same way, human lovers, true to the dynamic of twinning, must trade the power of Eros (cupid and arrow) back and forth to sustain the 'alchemical wedding' illustrated in the sixth Arcanum of the Tarot. (Crowley deck, from paintings by Frieda Harris, *far right bottom*)

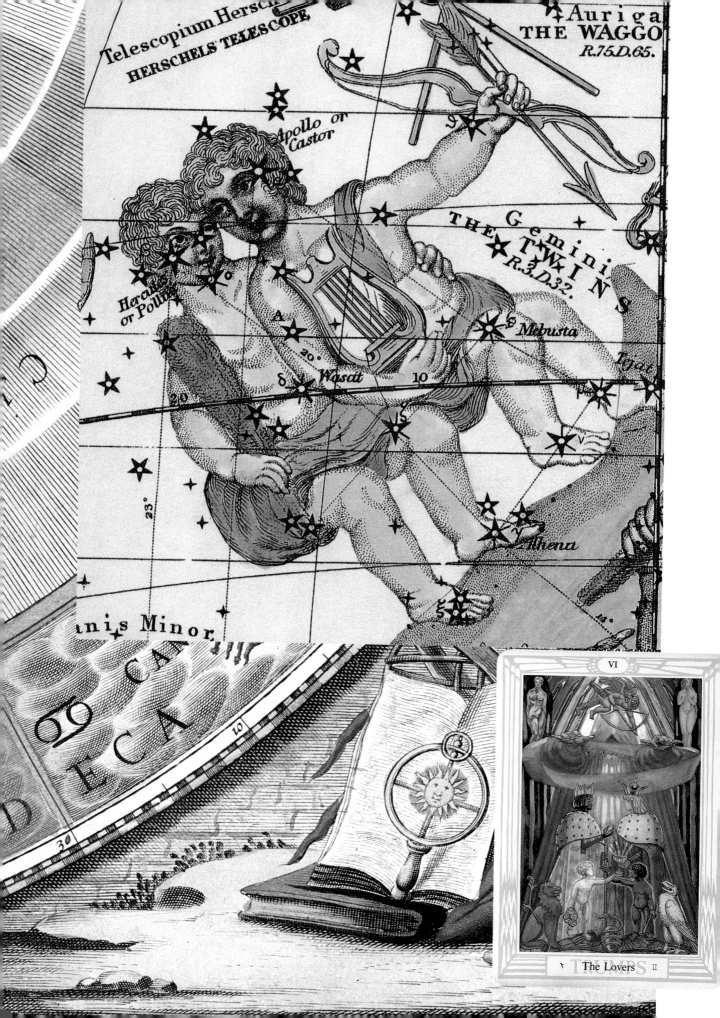

Telescopium Hersch

HERSCHELS TELESCOPE

Auriga
THE WAGGO
R.75.D.65.

Apollo or
Castor

G e m i n i s

THE
T W I N S
R.3.D.32.

Mebusta

Hercules
or Pollux

Tejat

Wasat

Athena

anis Minor.

69 CA

E CA

VI

The Lovers   II

As the embodiment of eternal duality, Twins readily suggest the allegorical pairing of Life and Death (Marten de Vos, *Allegory of Life and Death*, late 16th century), but this is not something to be understood merely as a logical proposition of mutual exclusion along Aristotelian lines: A is A, A is not B. In fact, the principle of logical identity is constantly contradicted or even violated in archaic and mythological forms of intuition which, to this day, see life and death as interfusing principles. Paradoxically, life is not opposed to death but the two are symbiotic. This implies that death is not merely the absence or negation of life but a counterforce that life needs in order to become what it is. The knowledge of death as an autonomous counterforce was one of the most closely guarded secrets of archaic shamanism and black magic, widely exploited in the native occultism of Central America. As Quetzalcoatl had his dark, death-dealing twin in Tezcatlipoca, so the life-force is twinned to the death-force, a self-regulating power with its own set of organic laws and critical boundaries. At the seam between the two, 'life' as we know it unfolds. (Clay figure representing eternal duality, Tlatico, Mexico, 1700–1350 BC)

The image of the divine androgyne may be viewed as a specific variant of the Twin. Iconizing the Decadent poet, Guillaume Apollinaire, as a sublime androgyne, Chagall is restating one of the favourite themes of his era, the transsexual self-sufficiency of the artist (Marc Chagall, *Homage to Apollinaire*, 1911). In this emblematic Valentine, including a heart pierced by an arrow (ancient cliché of Eros), Chagall certainly alludes to Apollinaire's notorious love affair with the Muse, She who uses the poet as a musician uses an instrument. He takes Adam and Eve as primordial androgyne Twins and recomposes them as Poet and Muse, She who holds the apple, He who playfully excites her sex; then he has Muse and Poet sing a duet. As the mandala-like structure of the background suggests, there is a grounding of One-and-Other but no final unity. Both life and art depend on how well we live, and love, the everlasting, evershifting play of Desire and Division.

The duplication of the human figure, found so often in archaic art and folk-loric motives, is not merely a decorative device. Paradoxically, Twins are the generative element of world-perception: not the unity of two-in-one but the dyadic structure of One-and-Other. (Gold foil figurines from Alaca Hüyäk, Turkey, 24,000–22,000 B C)

Genetics and Biological Twins

Biologically, the zygote (the product of the union of two reproductive cells) is the original twin parent of us all. The vast cell-complex composing the body of all sexually reproducing beings derives in its totality from the zygote, a perfect dyad, by a long series of successive divisions. The original cell first divides into two (mitosis), then these two into four, and so forth. With each division the amount of DNA doubles. As the organism becomes articulated, the twinning actions which generate it become more and more concealed. In the case of biological twins, however, the original zygotic cell is fully externalized. The degree of separation of Siamese twins is decided by the earlier or later splitting of the single zygotic unit. (*Above*: Illustration by Hans Driesch, 1891, and the original Siamese twins, Chang and Eng.)

Multiple births are viewed as a repetition of twinning: for instance, the Dione quintuplets result from a single zygote that twins and retwins, effectively cloning itself four times. Although the process has been studied intensely, the nine-banded armadillo is the only mammal in which the entire process of one-egg twinning has been thoroughly observed. (*Below*: four armadillo foetuses removed from the split-open single chorionic membrane, and painting by Franz Kupka.)

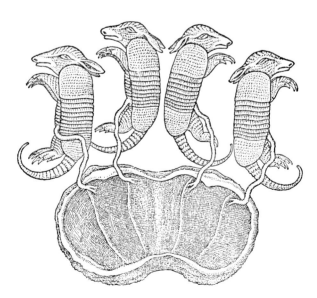

In primitive societies, the afterbirth exercises exceptional fascination and is often viewed as a double of the new-born. In this sense we all are born twins, connected by the left-hand-spiralling umbilicus to our biological Other. As the embodiment of the soul-double, the afterbirth is charged with *mana*, sacred power. In some cases, this power is attributed to the umbilicus itself. Rites of sacred kingship in central Africa, still practised in our time, include the birth cord in the ceremonial headgear. This resembles the Egyptian custom of showing the pharaoh with a 'bull's tail' hanging from his royal kilt, an image of the shrunken umbilicus as vestige of the double. This motif would have emphasized the avataric function of the pharaoh, who is at one and the same time himself and not himself: a human and, simultaneously, the vehicle of a superhuman principle, or living god (*neter*). (*Left and below*: Pharaoh with vestigial umbilicus, Seti I, c. 1300 BC; a new-born baby's umbilical chord.)

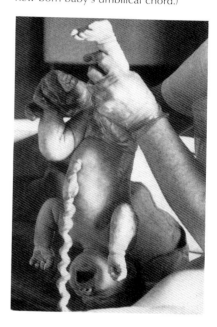

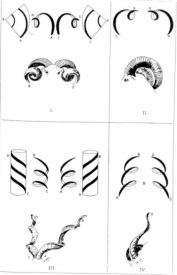

The Indo-European root, TWA-, basis of 'twin', also occurs in 'twine' and 'twilight'. Twine is a twisted thread, like DNA, the twine of nucleic acids which exhibits a consistent twinned structure and handedness. What for the archaic mind was imagined as twinning powers at the source of all life, for us appears in the scientific evidence of genetics. DNA acts to convert and deconvert the full spectrum of life-processes in nature and the human body and brain. Its counterpart, the messenger acid RNA, replicates (i.e., twins) the complex code of instructions embodied in the 'double helix' of DNA. (*Left and right*: homonymous curves on the ram's horns, and diagram of the double helix.)

First Parents and Ancestral Pairs

As totemic doubles who beget human offspring, the First Parents are often represented as ancestor-clones, such as the massive torsos of Easter Island. Judaeo-Christian myth reduces this feat of perpetual generation to the single creative act of God twinning the clone-wife Eve from Adam's own substance. (*Right*: from a 15th-century Book of Hours.)

The dyadic cosmology of the Egyptians describes Get raising Nut, an exact analogue of the modern concept of gravitation working against light, but inverted: Nut, the immaterial womb of

cosmic light which is paradoxically complete darkness, is raised and supported by the forces of the material earth. This demonstrates the implicit materialist bias of Egyptian cosmology, as well as the 'secret doctrine' that the earth (Geb) we inhabit acts as a founding-stone to support the extra-physical structure of the cosmos at large. Dyadic dynamism was inherent in the sacred geometry and engineering of the Egyptians, as well as other ancient cultures. (Papyrus of Tamienu, c. 1000 BC.)

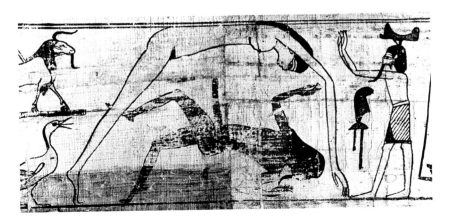

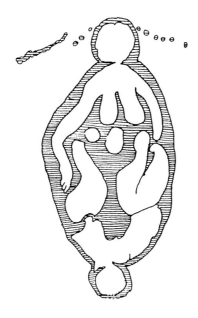

Primal incest among the gods was a generative, world-shaping act. Cosmic union of the Two in the world-egg is graphically pictured in Paleolithic figures engraved on stone. West Sudanese ancestor-twins and the two-headed ancestor effigy from Oceania demonstrate the same motif, for everywhere the First Parents were viewed as Twins. These images are tabu, revered for their embodiment of sacred power. (*Above:* engraved Stone Age figures, Laussel, France; ancestor figure from New Ireland; ancestor figure from Mali.)

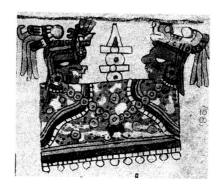

Judaeo-Christian tradition, by contrast, views incest as a sin and nothing more. With Lot and his daughter, its sacred meaning no longer applies in any sense. Christian doctrine asserts the pure individuality of each soul, unlike archaic psychology for which the soul is a fluidic element of nature, more like a bubble in a stream than the source of the stream. In this view, incest signifies intimate functions of twinning which may have, in time past, involved close interbreeding under ritual conditions.

Ever true to its origins, the psyche will periodically retrieve its lost content, and so the repressed or disregarded incest motif figures prevalently in alchemy, and in the archaic cosmology of the Aztecs where the First Parents are depicted, face to face, in a ceremonial casket emblematic of coitus, death and resurrection. The intercourse of the First Pair is eternal – if anything is. (*Above: Lot and his Daughters* by Altdorfer; and *left* an Aztec Codex showing the first couple with the Tree of Life.)

Totemic Doubles

When modern science proposes that human beings possess in the code-structure of DNA a genetic memory of all previous stages of animal evolution, it is merely restating what is, for archaic and mythological thinking, perfectly obvious. For aboriginal humanity, our parents were animals. The totem carries the racial identity in the same way that the genome carries individual identity. Totemic ancestors are therefore the supernatural doubles of all their offspring.

The great ancestor figures of Easter Island (*above*) resemble a line of clones all propagated from a single strain. Here the totemic identity of the primal ancestor stands as a monumental presence, enduring through time by a process of endless duplication. The same fact of nature – for it is to the primitive mind a given fact – is depicted vertically in the totem poles of the American Northwest. Salmon, raven, beaver, bear and other totemic doubles are here integrated with their human offspring in an unbroken continuity. Among the Mochica, ancestral origins go back to twin brothers who mated with twin women they first encountered in the form of parrots, or macaws. (Left: North American totem-pole; and Mochica stirrup vessel with two parrots perched on the head.)

The sacred presence and inspiration of the ancestral totem animals supports and directs the life of the clan. For this we appear to have adopted the DNA double helix as the 'totem pole' for the human species as a whole.

Beyond the general relation of the ancestral double to its clan, there is the possibility for a more specific relationship between individual and totem. This occurs in the shamanic practices of ritual trance and shapeshifting, when the powers of the totem are released through ecstatic and magical workings. Identity is fluidically exchanged between the shaman and the double, called *uay* or *nahual*. In a spirit double like the Hopi Katchina, the fluidic *mana* (sacred power) of the supernatural coalesces into a tangible form so that it can be employed in prayer and ritual. (Maya ruler wearing jaguar costume; and Hopi mask from Arizona.)

A third and very special condition of totemic doubling takes place in Tibetan religion, which exhibits trace remnants of archaic theocracy, rulership by the gods or their direct descendants. In Egyptian religion, the Pharaoh was a genetic carrier who doubled for an avataric being. The Pharaoh bore the 'god-self' as porters carry a potentate in his palanquin. Likewise, Tibetan Buddhism, derived in part from Bon Po shamanism, preserves a similar technique in the *tulku* (literally, 'altar'), the person who inherits the spirit of a reincarnating lama: hence the entitling of the Dalai Lama, the immaculate alter ego, in successive persons, 1st, 2nd, 3rd, etc. The Dalai Lama is a 'double agent', the current one being the 14th in a sequence of *tulkus*, a living totem or 'incarnate god' (*lha*). (The 14th Dalai Lama in 1942.)

Animal Powers

In Europe, Celtic bards as late as the 6th century AD still sang of their previous incarnations as salmon and crow, as if it were a matter of course. The pagan societies of Europe lived in an atmosphere of archaic sensitivity to what is now being called 'interspecies' rapport. The witch had her familiars (usually the cat), animal powers which she commanded by potion and spell.

The most impressive accomplishment of Christianity in eradicating such practices was neither the religious nor political hegemonies it generated, but the colossal rupture from our natural origins.

Far back into pre-history, animal powers were experienced as grounding and informing all human faculties, and especially the higher faculties. In the funerary regalia of Tutankhamun – certainly one of the most ogled sacred objects in the world – vulture and serpent stand out clearly as indications of the special clairvoyant abilities rooted physiologically in the pituitary and pineal glands. These abilities were supposed to have been possessed by the Pharaonic families due to carefully regulated interbreeding (motif of incestuous twins). A stone hacha from Veracruz in Mexico illustrates a similar kind of deliberate facultative mutation. Here the seer incorporates the animal powers of the dolphin through release of latent faculties in the backbrain, or cerebellum, often called the reptile- or fish-brain. (15th-century woodcut of a witch; Breton woodcarving; ancient Mexican hacha with dolphin crest.)

These motifs are freely repeated in Amerindian and Eskimo art of shamanic origins. Whether the power animal is a bird, represented in a mask, or a shaman shown in dialogue with its animal double, the bear, the meaning is the same: human knowledge alone is not enough to sustain and direct us in this world. (*Left*: funerary mask of Tutankhamun. *Above and right*: Goddess Hathor and Pharaoh Psammetichus I; Eskimo bird mask; North American raven mask; red stone pipe bowl from East Dakota.)

Demonic Doubles, Realm of the Nightmare

In its metamorphic aspect, the Twin becomes the Double, an entity capable of assuming a wide range of monstrous and nightmarish forms. Although the Double may also be benevolent, acting as an 'ally' to its original, the terms of this amicable and cooperative arrangement are anything but clear. The Jekyll/Hyde split is the most universally affecting example of the demonic double, as attested by the dozens of film remakes of R.L. Stevenson's classic tale. In the same vein, Frankenstein's monster can be viewed as a Jungian shadow-figure, the monstrous double of scientific materialism, originally envisioned by Shelley's wife Mary. (*Right*: illustration to *Dr. Jekyll and Mr. Hyde*, 1930; and poster for a film developing the *Frankenstein* theme.)

Our attachment to the exclusional unity of the personal ego – 'I am myself and I alone' – is challenged every night when the ego dissolves into the shifting miasma of the dream state – or partially dissolves, at least. Since Freud

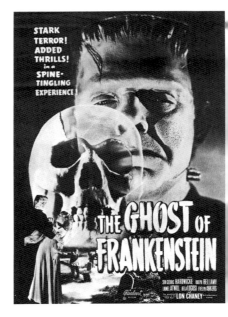

published *The Interpretation of Dreams* in 1900, it has become commonplace to view dream-images as animated fragmentations of the psyche. Like a face seen in a shattered mirror, the psyche can generate multiple images similar to the demonic familiars evoked deliberately in the practice of

witchcraft and shamanism. (Fuseli, *The Nightmare*, 1781, *below left*.) When the same thing happens in full waking, it results in the hallucinations of schizophrenia, chillingly and wittily captured by Max Ernst in his Surrealist sequence, *Une Semaine de bonté* (*below*).

Both symbolically and genetically, blood is identity. Therefore the loss of identity and the schizoid breakdown of the ego can produce, at its extreme, the manifestation of the bloodsucking Double, the vampire. As noted in connection with native Mexican occultism, archaic magic recognizes the autonomy of the 'death force' as equal to the life-force and not merely the result of its absence. The vampire is an entity who concentrates the death-force in a pseudo-vital condition that must be continually replenished by violating natural boundaries and consuming the blood of others. In fact, the vampire is a Double which has vanquished its original Other; therefore it has no reflection. (Edvard Munch's *The Vampire*, 1898; poster for *Le Frisson des Vampires*, 1971; and for *Dracula*, 1958.)

Metamorphosis of the Soul

Although the Western sense of personal ego as a fixed and exclusive unit precludes the primitive intuition of fluidic identity, we remain fascinated by the possibilities of psychic and spiritual metamorphosis. The soul, we believe, is like a butterfly in its cocoon stage. The supreme image of its full-blown maturity is the Risen Christ who, in another aspect of twinning, serves as the sacrificial double for humankind as a whole. (*Right*: Matthias Grünewald, *Resurrection*, c. 1510.)

Theologically, the Resurrection is a kind of totalitarian image which can cancel our appreciation of the other possibilities of transformation inherent to the soul. These are still remembered

and enacted in aboriginal cultures where mask and costume allow the celebrant to slip into the identity of a supernatural being. Ritual impersonation is not merely a game of play-acting, but an occasion for the soul-forces not confined to the exclusional ego to assume other forms and even reach into other worlds. Mimesis at this level is dramatic twinning, the experience of living the two-as-one. Fleeting dream images and the idle fantasies of daydreaming also demonstrate the soul's tendencies to transform and renew itself through passing over into the Other – momentarily, at least. Even death, the final and radical transformation, is imagined as the release of the soul-double into another realm of life, hopefully free of its human faults and limitations. (Blake: *Death of the Strong Wicked Man*, 1808.)

19th century. His manner of using colour often seems to simulate the impression of ectoplasmic substance at large in the atmosphere. His haunting portrait of a pubescent girl (*bottom right*) shows her ectoplasmic double as an ominous dark blob extruding from her side – significantly, from the location of the spleen, where vital force is said to be stored in a concentrated form, according to occult teachings of which Munch was certainly aware. Devitalization through the draining effects of the double was a fashionable theme in the art and literature of his time, as was also the opposite phenomenon, the regenerative transformation of the soul. (*Bottom left:* Illustration by Heinrich Vogeler of a 1914 edition of the Oscar Wilde fairy-tale 'The Fisherman and His Soul', 1888.)

Maya masks (*above*) reflect the confluence of living and dead. Certainly the most extreme and graphic example of soul metamorphosis occurs when the trance medium extrudes the so-called ectoplasmic double which may then assume the form of a departed person and speak to witnesses on the physical plane. Such manifestations have been photographed (*right*) many times, and occasionally in a convincing manner.

The Norwegian painter Edvard Munch lived during the heyday of such spiritualistic feats, at the end of the

Warring and Rivalry among Twins

In Greco-Latin myth, a famous set of rival twins is associated with the foundation of Rome. Among the kings of Alba Longa, in the pre-Roman era, there arose a factional dispute between two brothers, the younger of whom seized the throne. He placed his daughter, Rhea Silvia, in the sanctuary of the Vestal Virgins, but she was raped by the god Ares and gave birth to twins, Romulus and Remus. The king ordered the boys to be drowned following the age-old tabu against twins, but they were found and suckled by a she-wolf. Later, they were discovered by the royal herdsman who gave them into the care of his wife. When it came time for the founding of Rome, Romulus ploughed a furrow to establish the city boundary, and Remus impetuously jumped over it, for which transgression he was killed by his brother.

In Egyptian myth, a similar rivalry between Horus and Set results in establishing the unification of upper and lower Egypt. In typical paradoxical fashion, Twins can generate order or disrupt it. They can agree to disagree or agree to agree. Their conflict may result in the establishment of boundaries or, just as well, the disruption of them. In this precarious off-balance state, human affairs are often decided, so it can be said that many conditions in our world arise as consequences of momentary power-shifts between Twins. (Detail from Rubens' *Romulus and Remus*; Horus and Set, from the throne of Sesostris I, c. 1920 BC.)

The same applies for the on-again, off-again alliances between twin rivals who are represented mutually as tricksters. The Iroquois describe Hahgwehdiju as a benefactor from whom all good things come, while his twin brother, Hahgwehdaetgah, is a malefic spirit, responsible for poisonous plants, snakes and the like. Another variant among the Indians of the Northeast is Gluskap, who is opposed by Malsum, his younger twin. In both cases, both of the twins are tricksters who furiously compete in outsmarting each other, and the outcome of their contests decides the order of our world. Generally, there is no predicting whether the relations between Twins will be hostile or amicable, but hostility usually prevails. This confusion, once again, derives directly from the ambivalent value of the sacred. Whatever has numinous power can work either way, to harm or to heal, even to heal what it has harmed in the first place, or vice versa!

In the *Popol Vuh* of the Maya, the relations between the trickster twins, Hunaphu and Ixbalanque are generally cooperative, but Tezcatlipoca and Quetzalcoatl in Aztec myth are clearcut adversaries, as are Cain and Abel in the Biblical creation-myth. (*Above*: Maya twin symbols; and Quetzalcoatl dancing before Tezcatlipoca, Codex Borbonicus. *Below*: William Blake, *The Body of Abel found by Adam and Eve*.)

Scapegoat and Sacrifice

Sacrifice (literally, 'power-making') is the use of twinning for the transference and perpetuation of *mana*, sacred force. It is the most efficient exploitation of the dyadic nature of the Sacred. In order for this sacrifice to be effective, there must be a complete substitution or transference of identity. In the Biblical scapegoat, the animal is spattered with blood, invested with the sins of the community and driven into the wilderness. Scapegoating is the most potent mechanism of expurgation known to humanity. (*Above: The Scapegoat* by William Holman Hunt, 1856.)

As the supreme sacrifice, the Crucifixion is prepared by an elaborate set of events involving twins, substitutes and sacrificial doubles. The infant Jesus, even still in the womb, is twinned with his precursor, John the Baptist, as shown in Dürer's woodcut of Elizabeth, the mother of John, greeting Mary. The Gospel relates that the Jesus child leapt in the womb at the proximity of its counterpart. The

frequent depiction in Medieval and Renaissance art of Jesus and John together as infants recapitulates this theme; or it may perhaps illustrate the more esoteric concept that there were two distinct children called Jesus, descended from the two distinct genealogies found in the New Testament. (Dürer, *The Visitation*; and Bronzino, *The Holy Family with St Anne and John the Baptist*.)

Human sacrifice, whether in the case of Abraham and Isaac or among the Aztecs (Florentine Codex), has the simple aim of the transference or preservation of sacred power – the life-force being the most obvious and accessible aspect of the Sacred. In flaying, sacrificial twinning assumes a bizarre form in which the priest literally slips into the skin of the victim, becoming two-in-one. The victim is ritually honoured before sacrifice, often for a whole year, to develop a charge of sacred power, as it were; then, with the flaying, this charge is transferred to the priest and released through ritual and dance for the benefit of the entire community. Curiously, Jesus in the Gnostic Gospels described his own crucifixion in mystical terms as a regenerating dance. (Abraham sacrificing Isaac, from the synagogue of Beth Alpha; a Maya drawing of human sacrifice; and a Xipe Totec sculpture from Mexico showing a young man wearing the skin of a flayed human.)

Tabu and Fetish

Christendom is centrally concerned with the tabu on twins in the story of Esau and Jacob, the twin sons of Isaac and Rebekah. The Bible refers to their rivalry even while in the womb, a common twin-motif. In Benjamin West's painting both sons are proudly displayed to their father by two handmaids of Rebekah, with no apparent favour shown to one over the other. However, the custom of primogeniture ensures that the twins will be rivals and one will carry *tabu*, the ambivalence of blessed/cursed. It is the first-born and stronger, Esau, who is designated to receive the father's blessing, even though Jacob is spiritually destined to carry out the mission of his people. As the Bible tells it, Jacob must contrive to be chosen for his father's blessing because he has already been so chosen by God. Through the figure of Jacob, then, a superhuman and occult force intervenes in the natural state of affairs (transmission of paternal authority by primogeniture). Jacob is tabu redeemed. (*Above*: Benjamin West, *Isaac Being Shown His Twin Sons, Esau and Jacob*.)

Likewise, whenever twins are born in archaically rooted cultures, one twin is seen as an intervention of the supernatural into the natural world. As the blatant manifestation of the Other, one twin is supercharged with *mana*, or magical force. It is viewed as too dangerous to manage and must be eliminated. With alarming arbitrariness, one of the two is chosen to live and the 'other' is killed. This practice, although widespread, is by no means universal. Some communities in Africa today, such as the Yoruba, consider the life of their society to be dependent upon the periodic appearance of twins and both are honoured. Twin-fetishes are devised to control their occult force. (Twin-figure from Yorubaland; and BaLuba neckrest with twin figures.)

In Bali, each twin is called the 'betrothed' and the two are viewed in a special sense as lovers. In India twins are abhorred because of a fear of incest in the womb, such as Plutarch describes in his account of Isis and Osiris. Incest tabu which usually accompanies twins can be read two ways: as a warning against intertribal mating among the common people, and as an insurance of selective incest in the rites of sacred kingship. This is the specific 'double message' of twin effigies, for instance, on a Nigerian ancestor screen. Current studies in ethology have demonstrated beyond question the role of limited incest in animal speciation – yet another startling confirmation of the accuracy of primitive intuition.

In Europe, the twin-tabu has been often associated with the omen of 'monstrous births'. The two-headed Siamese twin in a British pamphlet of 1642 is fancifully pictured with a set of Hindu third eyes, periwigs, an Elizabethan collar, and feathers or snake-tails extruding from the elbows.

Anatomically, a two-headed body appears as a result of an extremely late twinning division. This feat of nature is so monstrous that it ignites the imagination to its own monstrous distortions. Beyond being a 'freak of nature', twins are the pretext for wild embellishment and prognostication of evil fortunes about the land. Their tabu is discharged into the atmosphere as a

mood of catastrophe and political strife. While Castor and Pollux were viewed in pagan Europe as saviour gods, the twin here becomes an apparition of evil happenings from which the people must, somehow or other, be rescued. (*Above*: ancestor screen from Nigeria. *Below*: Siamese twins in an English pamphlet of 1642; and Congolese image stuck with pins.)

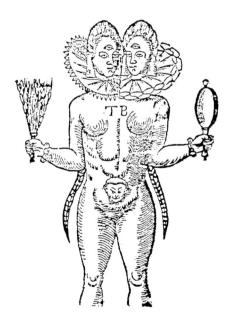

Androgynes and the Sexual Dyad

In the androgyne the perennial 'battle of the sexes' seems to be resolved, but is this an actual or merely an ideal, hoped-for resolution? Siamese twins do in fact appear, in the rarest of cases, where both members are hermaphroditic. This is perhaps nature's closest approximation of the perfect Twin in a single body.

Certain images in alchemical manuscripts of the Middle Ages could almost pass for anatomical drawings of Siamese twins, but it would be a mistake to impute such a literal, biological origin to these arcane creations. The archetype of perfect twinhood, combining both sexes into a single form and figure, is as old as any we know. It appears in figurines from Old Europe of 6000 BC, where a female form with sumptuous hips merges imperceptibly into an upright phallus, so that the hips readily become transformed into testicles and it is impossible to tell, finally, if the figure is either phallic or yonic. Here is the androgynous Twin in its original metamorphic splendour.
(Hermaphrodite, woodcut of 1550; decoration on a Pueblo bowl, c. 900 AD; and prehistoric figurine from Yugoslavia, c. 6000 BC.)

The same merger of phallic and yonic traits becomes completely stylized in the Hindu votive shrine composed of lingam and yoni. Here our twin-sexed physiological structure is celebrated as the source and fountainhead of all creation: the Cosmos is dyadic. Worship of the generative powers always took into account the bisexual or androgyne nature of human sexual design. The two sexes are perceived by primitive intuition as we see facing profiles and chalice in the well-known optical trick of figure-ground reversal. The sexes are dissimilar but indissolvable, not a unity but a dyadic unit. Today we are still fascinated by the flux and interchange of sexual personae without, perhaps, sensing the presence of the sacred within the play of ambiguities. (*Above*: lingam set in the yoni, Himachal Pradesh, 18th century. *Left*: photo of Andrew Logan.)

Lovers and Soul-Mates

Great epics of the European Middle Ages were often tales of fate-bound lovers who demonstrate a twin-like dynamic, even if they are not twins by biological definition. Both Teutonic and Anglo-Saxon classics attest to the curious syndrome of *tvillingelov*, 'twin-love'. It describes the uncanny bond between two partners in an action or drama who cannot exhibit, as individuals, the necessary strength to act alone. Then, because they are unable, acting as a pair, to undo the bond between them, the results of their mutual actions are often tragic.

Twin-love has been idealized and iconicized in all cultures through the ages. From the earliest surviving images, such as the 'Gumelnita lovers' from the East Balkans, down to the rhapsodic coupling of Rodin's *'Eternal Idol'*, the same possibility is restated. Surely it is Eros, rather than Hope, that springs eternal in the human breast. (Prehistoric figures, East Balkans, 5th millennium BC; Nepalese statuette showing the Adibuddha Vajradhara in union with his Sakti; and Rodin, *The Eternal Idol*.)

Eros and Strife, Desire and Division, are the ever-present powers of twinning. In theology, the question of human ensoulment rests upon a dyadic premise of soul and body as twins, and this premise carries over directly into romantic psychology. Gottfried of Strassbourg, author of the best version of *Tristan and Isolde*, may have earned the Church's disapproval for the bold trope in which he compared the lovers' passion to the sacrament of the Holy Mass, thereby enshrining eroticism in the sanctuary of religion. Erotic interfusion can be torturous as well as delightful. The love-death of Delville's soul-twins is the horizontal, tragic version of Rodin's prayerful, ascending kiss. (*Left*: J. Delville, *Tristan and Yseult*, 1887.)

Oriental iconic idealizations of Duality, such as the yab-yum, express the metaphysical abstraction by which the duad is resolved, or seemingly so. Western equivalents to the Tantric embrace can be found in the alchemical 'water-marriage' and the conjugal bath of the First Parents in a Mayan codex. Medical science demonstrates that slivers of heart-cells in separate Petri dishes will beat at their own rates, but placed in proximity in the same dish, they will synchronize beating. The will-to-merge informs all conjugations of twinning, mythic, romantic and biological. (*Below*: water-marriage from an alchemical treatise, 1624; and the conjugal bath of the First Parents from a Mayan codex.)

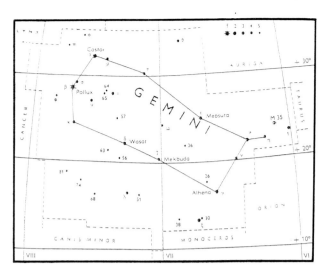

Heavenly Twins

The constellation of the Twins, known by the Latin term, *Gemini*, is clearly visible in the night sky from autumn to late spring. Schematically, it consists of two elongated figures marked by a pair of bright stars named after the Dioscuri, 'Sons of Zeus', Castor and Pollux. In pictorial versions of the constellation, they are usually designated as the head stars of the Twins, but in some cases they mark their throats or shoulders. (*Above*: a

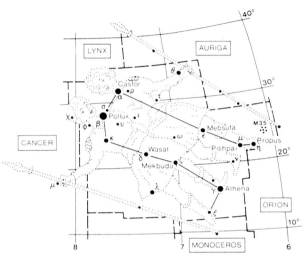

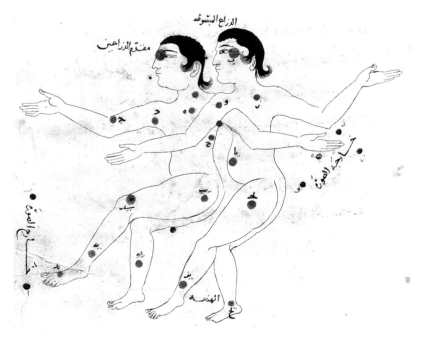

French 16th-century calendar. *Left*: an Arabian engraved mirror, 13th century.)

Sidereal twin lore is so immensely rich that images of the pair can be found in hundreds of variants from a dozen or so cultures. In some cases, such as the *Book of Fixed Stars* by Abd ar-Rahman al-Sufi, there is an attempt to preserve a clear and accurate relation between the figures, their gestures and the actual star positions, but in most cases this conformity is lost or ignored, allowing for considerable artistic license. (*Above*: a modern star-map, and a reconstruction of an English work of the 8th century. *Left*: from the *Book of Fixed Stars* by Abd ar-Rahman al-Sufi.)

As the best known of all Western Twin variants, Castor and Pollux were widely revered in sanctuaries all around the Mediterranean. The cult of the divine twins finds its oldest prototype in the Ashvins of the *Rig Veda*, charioteers connected with lightning, fertility and travel. The mytheme was readily assimilated into Christianity as well. In the Syriac *Acts of Thomas* the brother of Jesus, Thomas or Judas Thomas, was regarded as a twin. Empowered through his divine counterpart, he performs wonders like those of the Dioscuri. Even the two apostles, John and James, seem to have taken on the motif. In Gnostic lore they are called *Boanerges*, 'Sons of Thunder', and invested with pagan twin attributes. (*Right*: an English astronomical tract, 14th century.)

The Twins appeared regularly on astrological charts and illustrations dividing the year by the signs of the Zodiac. (*Below*: Relief by Agostino di Duccio, Rimini; a German woodcut 1515; mosaic from Beth Alpha Synagogue.)

Mirrors and Optical Illusions

The optical illusion of facing profiles, black on a white background, which become the outline of a chalice, white on a black background, illustrates twinning twice-over: the profiles face to face are twins to each other, and the facing profiles, taken as a set, are twin to the chalice. In the first case the two profiles are mirror twins; in the second case, profiles and chalice are metamorphic twins. The elusive visual conversion from one to other (known as 'figure-ground reversal', introduced in 1915 by Edgar Rubin for use in perceptual studies) demonstrates the shifty, fluidic power of Twins. The metamorphic shift from profiles to chalice and vice-versa can be neither controlled nor anticipated.

The minor lore of mirrors is large and widespread, surviving to this day in the common superstition that it is unlucky to break a mirror. Divination by mirrors (catoptromancy) is attested by Pausanius, who described a sacred well near Patras where, when someone who was ill let down a mirror on a string so that it barely touched the surface of the water, a picture of the outcome of their illness would appear in the mirror. Paradoxically, the mirror-surface which carries the image of desire also separates us from it, as clearly revealed in the tale of the dog who is tempted by his own reflection to drop the bone he is holding. (Franz Cleyn, illustration to Aesop, 1665, and (*left*) Escher's *Relativity*, 1953.)

It takes some powerful impulsion, rising from the realm beneath conscious will and thought, to be transported through the looking-glass, like Alice. Generally, our relation to Duality is quite external and superficial and when, on occasion, we engage it more deeply, the world truly turns topsy-turvy. Curiously, there is almost no positive magical lore connected with mirrors. The land attained through the looking-glass is full of tests and terrors. (Two illustrations by John Tenniel from *Alice Through the Looking-Glass*.)

Human narcissism, hard to resist and even harder to break, is a perilous flirtation with the Other in the guise of oneself. Most evidence strongly attests that shifting the boundaries between One and Other throws us into a world of radical disorientation. Possibly the one exception is the case of the Japanese Sun-Goddess, Amaterasu, who is lured from hiding in a cave by the reflection of her own radiance in a mirror. (Photograph by Ed van der Elsken; Max Kluger, *Vom Tode II*; and a Japanese print of the Sun Goddess emerging from the cave.)

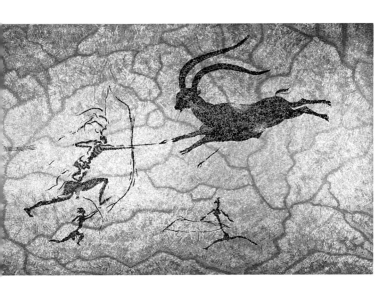

Imitative Twinning, Magical Duplication

Considered anthropologically, the cliché, 'A picture is worth a thousand words,' may be viewed as expressing a rather late and decadent stage of human culture. In *illo tempore*, that magical time of beginnings cited in so many primitive myths, a picture was worth the thing itself. This epoch of human evolution seems to have

culminated in the Upper Paleolithic, around 30,000 BC, leaving as its testament the magnificent cave-paintings of Southern France and the Spanish Pyrenees. Archaic mentality knew the meaning of 'animation' in a way that continues today, perhaps, only in the way children experience the creatures in animated cartoons. (*Top*: paintings from two of the prehistoric caves in Spain.)

Imitative magic is generative and dynamic, not merely a passive mimicry. Since identity is fluid and metamorphic, the shaman-hunter at Les Trois Frères (*above*) becomes what he imitates. The

dance, the mask, the image or name, do not merely *represent* the object or entity, they *present* the double of the object or entity, fully as alive and potent as the original.

Wherever imitative magic is employed, appeasement and manipulation of sacred powers use picture-doubles, masks, petroglyphs and puppets, such as the scare-devil from the Nicobar Islands; in voodoo, hair and nail-cuttings which duplicate the person targeted for a spell. (*Above right*: scare-devil from the Nicobar Islands. *Left*: medieval English jug containing pins, hair and nail parings.)

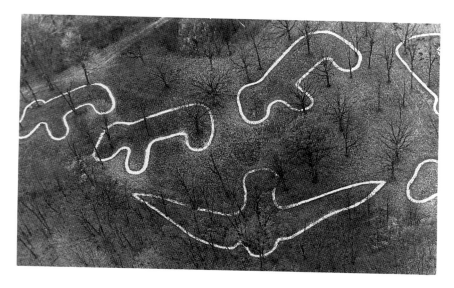

In Pre-Columbian America, animal silhouettes incised in the earth are as alive as their natural counterparts. (*Left:* the Marching Bear Mound Group, Iowa.)

Among the Aranda of Australia the *tjurunja* is a clan-totem and tool of imitative magic, repository of clan history and ancestral spirit. Levy-Bruhl reported that the *tjurunja* is also taken as the exact double of each individual in the clan, i.e., as a multiple twinning or cloning device. Handling it in the sacred ceremony, the Aranda say, 'This is my body,' an exact parallel to the words pronounced in the Christian mass when the Host is administered: 'Take, eat, this is my body.' (*Right:* two Australian *tjurunjas*; and a Lutheran painting of the Sacraments.)

Imitative magic of this kind is widespread today more in its profane than its sacred aspects: for instance, in advertising. An advert for men's cologne (*left*) uses the motif of desire-and-division to arouse an initial response. The desire-object, a woman (as usual), is divided from the male by some unnameable divisive power which can, however, be overcome if the male performs a rite of imitation using the cologne as a totemic device to transfer his sexual power from the realm of the imaginary into the realm of the actual. The unattainable woman portrayed is the double of a real-life woman who can be possessed. Likewise, the name and image of the cologne are the source of magical duplications which can produce the effect of the original product – or they had better, otherwise the advert will be discontinued! Thus the magical efficacy of a totem is attached to 'name-brands' which are touted in ferocious competitions of imitative magic.

Light and Darkness, Sun and Moon

Dyadic structure is often correlated to universal principles such as light and darkness, spirit and matter, life and death, etc. When this occurs, the tension or disparity between the two polar components will persist in some manner, so that the dyadic character clearly overrides any tendencies toward harmonic unification. The Dyad is non-resolving, hence its generative power. Light and dark are continually displacing each other, competing like the two different profiles of a face. (*Right*: Quetzalcoatl as Lord of Life and Lord of Death, Huastec sculpture, Mexico.)

According to Goethe's theory of light, the interplay of the Twins, Light and Dark, produces all the colours as a field of unstable colloidal states. Sun and Moon, likewise, are an uneven match, locked in a see-saw action often illustrated emblematically in alchemical writings. (*Below left*: an alchemical treatise of 1617.)

The curious term 'spagyric', used by some alchemical adepts, describes the clash of whirling vortices that intersect and spill through each other, generating the perpetual tide-change of inner turmoil that occupies the 'inner

space' within dense materiality. This plenum of exquisite reciprocal tensions seems to have been rediscovered in the realm of 'chaos'. (*Below right*: woodcut from T. Norton's *Ordinall of Alchemy*, 1662.)

The battle of light and darkness within the human psyche assumes figurative expression in Twins as well. Whether these be the two aspects of Quetzalcoatl, or the frightening multiplication of doubles in Hödler's matched paintings, *Day* and *Night*, (*above*) the odd, unsettling impression is the same. Duality is as inescapable as the split between dreaming and being awake. Hödler's figures stretch and stir in Castaneda's fabled 'crack between the worlds'. (*Left*: Pueblo bowl painted with human figures, New Mexico.)

Further Reading

Ambesi, Alberta Cesare, *Oceanic Art*, London, 1970.

Bazin, Germain, *The Avant-Garde in the History of Painting*, London, 1969.

Bihalji-Merin, and Tomasevic, Nebojao-Bato, *World Encyclopedia of Naive Art*, London, n.d.

Bodleian Picture Books, 13; *Islamic Constellations*, Oxford, n.d.

Burland, Cottie, *The Aztecs*, London, 1975

——*Mythology of the Americas*, London, 1968.

Campbell, Joseph, *Occidental Mythology*, London, 1965.

Carra, Masima, *Metaphysical Art*, London, 1971.

Cassou, Jean, *The Concise Encyclopedia of Symbolism*, London, 1984.

Cavendish, Richard, *The Book of Magic*, London, 1977.

Charbonneaux, Jean, Martin, Roland, and Villard, François, *Archaic Greek Art*, London, 1968.

Clive, Seymour, *Drawings of Rembrandt*, New York, 1965.

Copland, R., *The Kalender and Compost of Days (Paris, 1493)*, London, 1931.

Duval, Jean-Luc *Modern Art, 1884–1914*, Skira, 1979.

Eliade, Mircea, ed., *The Encyclopedia of Religion*, New York, 1972.

——*Myths, Dreams and Mysteries*, New York, 1967.

——*Patterns in Comparative Religion*, New York, 1958.

——*Shamanism: Archaic Technique of Ecstasy*, tr. W.R. Trask, Arkana, 1989.

Ellis Davidson, H.R., *Scandinavian Mythology*, London, 1969.

Ernst, Max, *Une Semaine de bonté*, Paris, 1963.

Fabricus, Johannes, *Alchemy*, London, 1976.

Frazer, Sir James, *Myths of the Origin of Fire*, London, 1930.

——*The Golden Bough*, London, 1890 and later reprints.

Gardner, Martin, *The Ambidextrous Universe*, Harmondsworth, 1964.

Gettings, Fred, *Encyclopedia of the Occult*, London, 1986.

——*The Book of the Zodiac*, London, 1972.

Gimbutas, Marija, *Goddesses and Gods of Old Europe*, London, 1982.

Girard, René, *Violence and the Sacred*, Baltimore and London, 1977.

——*Desire, Deceit and the Novel*, Baltimore, 1974.

——*Things Hidden from the Foundation of the World*, Baltimore, 1990.

——*The Scapegoat*, Baltimore, 1988.

Grant, Michael, *Roman Myths*, London, 1971.

Grant, M., and Hazel, J., *Who's Who in Classical Mythology*, London, 1983.

Harris, J. Rendell, *The Cult of Heavenly Twins*, Cambridge, 1906.

Haslam, Malcolm, *The Real World of Surrealism*, London, 1978.

Hastings, James, ed., *Encyclopedia of Religion and Ethics*, Edinburgh, 1911

Hawkes, Nigel, *Genetic Engineering*, Franklin Watts, 1991.

Johnson, Robert, *The Psychology of Romantic Love*, London, 1984.

Jullian, Philippe, *The Symbolists*, London, 1973.

Kagan, Andrew, *Marc Chagall*, New York, 1989.

Kerényi, Carl, *The Gods of the Greeks*, London, 1974.

Lackner, Stephan, *Max Beckman*, London, 1991.

Laing, R.D., *The Divided Self*, London, 1969.

Lévy-Bruhl, Lucien, *The "Soul" of the Primitive*, tr. L.A. Clare, London, 1938.

Morenz, Siegfried, *Egyptian Religion*, trans. Ann E. Keep, London, 1973.

Needham, Joseph, *Science and Civilization in China*, London, 1959, vol. III.

Newman, H.H., *Twins and Supertwins*, London, 1942.

Nicholson, I., *Mexican and Central American Mythology*, Middlesex, 1967.

Olschak, B.C., *Mystic Art of the Ancient Orient*, London, 1973.

Opie, Iona, and Tatem, M., *The Dictionary of Superstitions*, London, 1989.

Osborne, Harold, *South American Mythology*, London, 1968.

Paglia, Camille, *Sexual Personae*, London, 1992.

Perowne, Stewart, *Roman Mythology*, London, 1969.

Piggot, Juliet, *Japanese Mythology*, London, 1969.

Poignant, Roslyn, *Oceanic Mythology*, London, 1967.

Paltrinieri, M., and Radin, E., *The Book of Practical Astrology*, New York, 1981.

Reid, D.J., and Reid, A.E.K., *Human Biology*, 1987.

Russell, Jeffrey Burton, *A History of Witchcraft*, 1980.

Russell, John, *Max Ernst*, London, 1967.

Shepard, L., *Encyclopedia of Occultism and Parapsychology*, Detroit, 1991.

Shirley, Ralph, *The Mystery of the Human Double*, London, 1965.

Sieveking, Anna, *The Cave Artists*, London, 1979.

Sivapriyananda, Swami, *Astrology and Religion in Indian Art*, 1990.

Spence, Lewis, *Myths and Legends of Ancient Egypt*, London, 1915.

Tedlock, Dennis, *Popol Vuh*, New York, 1985.

Tompkins, Peter, *Secrets of the Great Pyramid*, London 1978.

Wallace, Marjorie, *The Silent Twins*, London, 1986.

Acknowledgments

Illustrations are acknowledged to the following collections and photographers with the following abbreviations: a above, b below, c centre, l left, r right:

Peter Adler Collection (photo Ian Skelton) 36–7; Ankara Museum (photo Josephine Powell) 65; Auckland Museum 43; Gernsheim Collection, Harry Ransom Humanities Research Center, The University of Texas at Austin 54; Basle: Museum für Völkerkunde und Schweizerisches Museum für Volkskunde 81b, (E. Eckert Collection, photo Peter Horner) 40, Öffentliche Kunstsammlungen 26; Photo Peter Bellwood 70a; Kunstmuseum, Berne 95a&c; Kruzat Kefzibah, Bet Alpha Synagogue 81al, 89br; British Film Institute, Stills, Posters & Designs 46, 47; The Brooklyn Museum, Henry L. Batterman and Frank S. Benson Funds 94a; Musées Royaux des Beaux-Arts de Belgique, Brussels (photo A.C.L., Brussels) 87a; Egyptian Museum, Cairo 58, 72br, 73al, (photo Hirmer Fotoarchiv) 78b; Fitzwilliam Museum, Cambridge 52; Peabody Museum, Harvard University, Cambridge, Massachusetts (photo Hillel Burger) 71ar; Remigia, Gasulla, Castellon 92al; Musée Unterlinden, Colmar (photo Marburg) 76a; Photo courtesy The Commercial Press (Hong Kong) Limited 42; National Museum, Copenhagen 37; Collection Van Abbemuseum, Eindhoven 64; Photo Ed van der Elsken, courtesy Institut Français, London 91cl; Goethe-Museum, Frankfurt 74bl; Goya International Ltd 93b; Bob Jones University, Greenville, South Carolina 82a; Haags Gemeentemuseum, The Hague 90l; Hamburgisches Museum für Völkerunde, Hamburg 69ac; Photo Irmgard Groth-Kimball 77al; Hulton Deutsch Collection Limited 66al&ar; London: British Library 24, British Museum 11, 12, 34, 38, 56, 57, 68b, 70bl, 76b, 82br, 83br, 86bl, 92cr, 93c (photo Edwin Smith) 41; Tate Gallery 48–49, 79b, The Trustee of the Wellcome Trust 72ar; Photo courtesy Centre for Kent Studies, Maidstone 30; Courtesy Marlborough Gallery, London 59; Maxwell Museum of Anthropology 95b; Photo Will McBride 87a; The Board of Trustees of the National Museums & Galleries on Merseyside (Liverpool Museum) 17, (Lady Lever Art Gallery, Port Sunlight) 80a; Mesa Verde National Park Museum, Colorado 84bl; Mexico: Instituto Nacional de Antropologia e Historia 23, Museo Nacional de Antropologia (photo Irmgard Groth-Kimball) 14; Ajit Mookerjee Collection 85r; © A.G. Müller, CH 8212 Neuhausen 61b; American Museum of Natural History, New York 4; Vojvodjanski Muzej, Novi Sad 6; Oltenita Archaeological Museum, Romania 86a; Nasjonalgalleriet, Oslo 77br; Canadian Museum of Civilisation, Ottawa, National Museums of Canada 37br; Oxford: Bodleian Library 88b, 89ar, Pitt Rivers Museum, University of Oxford 83a, 92b; Paris: Bibliothèque de l'Assemblée Nationale 79ar, Bibliothèque Nationale 68a, Musée Picasso (© photo R.M.N.) 55, Musée Rodin 86br; By kind permission of the Earl of Pembroke, Wilton House, near Salisbury, Wiltshire 33; Philadelphia Museum of Art, Louise and Walter Arensberg Collection 51; Courtesy of the Carnegie Museum of Natural History, Pittsburgh, Pennsylvania 73cr; Portland Art Museum 73ar; Narodni Galerie, Prague 66br; Private Collection 70br, (photo Irmgard Groth-Kimball) 72bl, 75al; *Psychic News* 77cr; Tempio Malatestiano, Rimini (photo Alinari) 89l; Photo Mick Rock 85l; Rome: Biblioteca Apostolica Vaticana 60al, 69b, 87br, Galleria Nazionale d'Arte Antica (photo Scala) 44; Pinacoteca Capitolina (Photo Alinari-Anderson) 78a; Church of San Giminiano (photo Studio Fontanelli) 20; Linden-Museum, Stuttgart 73br, 82bl; Museo Archeologico Nazionale, Syracuse 35; Regional Anthropological and Historical Museum, Villa Lermosa, Tabasco, Mexico 63; Santolea, Teruel 92a; Thyssen-Bornemisza Collection 45; Venator & Hanstein KG, Cologne 91cr; Basilica of San Marco, Venice (photo Osvaldo Böhm) 31; Vienna: Historisches Museum der Stadt Wien 53, Kunsthistorisches Museum 69c, 80br; Museum Rietberg, Zurich 69ar.

Illustrations have also been reproduced from the following publications: Lewis Carroll, *Alice's Adventures in Wonderland*, 1865, 91a, A. Cellarius, *Atlas Coelestis*, 1660 60r, Albrecht Dürer, *Die nördliche Himmelskugel*, 1515 89cr, Max Ernst, *Une Semaine de bonté*, 1934 74br, Michael Maier, *Atlanta fugiens*, 1617 94bl, Ulrich Molitor, *Tractatus von den bösen Weibern*, 1495 72al, H.H. Newman, *Twins and Super-Twins*, 1942 66bl, T. Norton, *Ordinall of Alchemy*, 1652 94br, J. Ogilvy, *Fables of Aesop paraphrased in Verse*, 1665 90br, R.L. Stevenson, *Dr Jekyll and Mr Hyde*, 1930 74al, Oscar Wilde, 'The Fisherman and His Soul', 1914 77bl, *De Alchimia Opuscula*, 1550 84a, *Newes from New-England*, 1642 83 bl.